Young Writers 2003 **WRITING COMPETITION FOR SECONDARY SCHOOLS**

T·A·L·E·S·

From The Midlands Vol II
Edited by Steve Twelvetree

Disclaimer

Young Writers has maintained every effort
to publish stories that will not cause offence.

Any stories, events or activities relating to individuals
should be read as fictional pieces and not construed
as real-life character portrayal.

Young**Writers**

First published in Great Britain in 2005 by:
Young Writers
Remus House
Coltsfoot Drive
Peterborough
PE2 9JX
Telephone: 01733 890066
Website: www.youngwriters.co.uk

All Rights Reserved

© *Copyright Contributors 2005*

SB ISBN 1 84602 316 5

Foreword

Young Writers was established in 1991 and has been passionately devoted to the promotion of reading and writing in children and young adults ever since. The quest continues today. *Young Writers* remains as committed to engendering the fostering of burgeoning poetic and literary talent as ever.

This year, *Young Writers* are happy to present a dynamic and entertaining new selection of the best creative writing from a talented and diverse cross section of some of the most accomplished secondary school writers around. Entrants were presented with four inspirational and challenging themes.

'Myths And Legends' gave pupils the opportunity to adapt long-established tales from mythology (whether Greek, Roman, Arthurian or more conventional eg The Loch Ness Monster) to their own style.

'A Day In The Life Of ...' offered pupils the chance to depict twenty-four hours in the lives of literally anyone they could imagine. A hugely imaginative wealth of entries were received encompassing days in the lives of everyone from the top media celebrities to historical figures like Henry VIII or a typical soldier from the First World War.

Finally 'Short Stories', in contrast, offered no limit other than the author's own imagination while 'Hold The Front Page' provided the ideal opportunity to challenge the entrants' journalistic skills, asking them to provide a newspaper or magazine article on any subject of their choice.

T.A.L.E.S. From The Midlands Vol II is ultimately a collection we feel sure you will love, featuring as it does the work of the best young authors writing today.

Contents

Anuj Patel (14) — 1

Beaumont Leys School, Leicester
Adam Smith (13) — 2

Belgrave High School, Tamworth
Rachel Cockram (12) — 3
Victoria Simpson (12) — 4
Kelly Day (12) — 5
Rebecca Scott (12) — 6
Dominic Hookey (12) — 8
Charlotte Stroud (12) — 10
Laura Black (12) — 12
Kirsty Sands (11) — 14
Ashleigh Williams (13) — 15
Thomas Hughes (13) — 16
Amy Williams (13) — 17
Emma Rees (12) — 18
Nathan Hill (11) — 19

Biddulph High School, (Specialist Sports College) Stoke-on-Trent
Kayleigh Williamson (14) — 20
Nathan Legg (15) — 21
Stacey Bennett (15) — 22
Katy Austin — 24
Jemma Goddard (14) — 25
Matthew Rowan (13) — 26
Jonathan Bailey — 27
Aaron Hulme (14) — 28
Chris Austin (14) — 29
Jacob Chell (14) — 30
Georgina Wright (14) — 31
Hannah Shaw (14) — 32
Hannah Leese (14) — 33

Countesthorpe College, Leicester

Emily Wilkinson (14)	34
Darren Wallis (14)	35
Sean Creasey (14)	36
Philip Nicholson (15)	37
Sam Hirst (14)	38
Carly Dolman (15)	39
Alex Marvin (15)	40
Steven Richards (14)	41

Elliott Durham School, Nottingham

Mitchell Wickes (12)	42
Sarah Lee (13)	44

Hope Valley College, Hope Valley

Elizabeth Taylor (12)	45
Sophie Kellett (12)	46
Hannah Stanish (12)	47
Anne-Marie Higgins (12)	48
Sarah Jenkins (12)	49
Tom Jolley (12)	50
Vanessa Morgan (12)	51
Jack Langley (11)	52
Rachel Taylor (12)	53
Rory Loveless (12)	54
Katie Brierley (12)	56
Richard Achahboun (12)	57
Jessica Slack (11)	58
Rebecca Harby (12)	60
Ellie Hepworth (12)	61
Sophie Carter (12)	62
Jake Hickinson (11)	64
Jordan Lilley (12)	65
Jonathan Swain (12)	66
Robert Barnatt (12)	67
Katie Hodges (12)	68
Bryony Pullman (12)	70

King Edward VI School, Lichfield

Jenny Benham (13)	71

Robbie Beck (13)   72
Liz Hollis (13)   73
Pippa Revell (13)   74
Holly Youlden (13)   75
Sam Atkins (13)   76
Robin Nowell (13)   77
Mat Wannell (13)   78
Harriet Thompson (13)   79
Megan Cross (13)   80
Stuart Clayton (13)   81

Kingsbury School, Tamworth
Laura Wheeler (12)   82
Robert Ovens (12)   83
Sarah Snazle (12)   84
Jessica Nash (12)   85
Holly Cant (12)   86
Reuben Butler (12)   87
Joe Coupe (12)   88
Ben Evans (11)   89
Steven Carter (12)   90
Danielle Purves (12)   91
Lucy Foster (12)   92
Jordan Hinds (12)   93
Keeley Humphries (12)   94
Charlotte Perry (12)   95
Freisha Patel (12)   96
Rhys Yates (12)   97

Kirkby College, Nottingham
Rebecca Jones (12)   98
Kallum Beazley (12)   99
Jay Roberts (13)   100
Drew Evans (12)   101
Alice Thoburn (12)   102

Leicester High School for Girls, Leicester
Anna Robinson (12)   104
Emma Boyd (11)   105
Susanna Goodhart (11)   106
Rebecca Twynham (12)   107

Sonal Shah (11)	108

Ludlow CE School, Ludlow
Joshua Taylor (13)	109
Hugh Williamson (13)	110

Manor High School, Leicester
Kieran Vyas (13)	111
Charlotte Fox (13)	112
Narisha Vora (13)	113
Rebecca Tobin (13)	114
Charu Thanvi (13)	115
Sonam Mehta (13)	116
Karishma Manji (13)	117
Shreena Sonecha (13)	118
Durga Gandhi (13)	119
Jemma Healey (13)	120

Maplewell Hall Special School, Loughborough
Tim Riches (14)	121
Helen Edwards (13)	122
Rhona McLean (15)	124
Robert Shirton (14)	125
Lisa James (16)	126
Sian Palmer (14)	127
Charlotte King (14)	128
Daniel Newbold (15)	129
Khan Dean (15)	130
Kirk Baker (15)	131
Lana Riches (15)	132
Alix Moore (12)	133
Leah Wright (12)	134
Emily Golding (16)	135
Jakob Whiten (13)	136
Jason Hadley (14)	137
Dannielle Thornton (12)	138

St Benedict's RC School, Derby
Maria Brown (13)	139
Thomas Wilkinson (13)	140

Adam Fraczek (13)	141
Ben Bullivant (13)	142
Natalie Barratt (13)	143
Katie McCabe (12)	144
Olivia McCalla (12)	145
Grace Greene-Gallagher (12)	146
Maeve Nethercott (12)	147
James Varney (12)	148
Ted Kemplen (12)	149
Mark Roe (13)	150
Ashleigh Warman-Dawes (12)	151
Heather Cripps (11)	152
Matthew Regan (12)	153
Anna Cripps (13)	154
Christopher Ruston (12)	155
Jessica Kate Coupland (12)	156
Aisling Lammond (12)	157
Tom Hall (12)	158

St Mary's RC High School, Hereford

Lucy Windall (12)	159
Lucie Rivers (11)	160
Natasha MacMahon (12)	161
Dominic Wylor-Owen (14)	162
James Pember (13)	163
Alex Caine (14)	164
Natasha James (12)	165
Stacey Hirst (11)	166
Maysie Williams (12)	167
Joseph Langley (11)	168
Daniel Tanner (12)	169
Daniel Winter (12)	170
Kate Probert-Jones (12)	171
Bronwyn Townsend (12)	172
Amalie Millest (13)	173
Emily Lunn (12)	174
Kathryn Martin (13)	175
Samantha Earnshaw (12)	176
Frances Lloyd (11)	177
Antonia Morgan (12)	178
Rebecca Lovelock (12)	179

Aniela Neicho (12)	180
Johan van Meeuwen (12)	181
Alex Thomas (12)	182
Rebecca Gilling (12)	183
Catherine Leslie (13)	184
Eva Howard (13)	185
Kimberley Langford (13)	186
Harriet Chapman (12)	187
Fábio Anselmo (12)	188
Rachel Ingram (14)	189
Lloyd Collins (13)	190
Mollie Russell (12)	191
Julianne Clark (13)	192
Isabel Fawcett (12)	193
Josie Walters (13)	194
Adam Powell (13)	195
Amber Gray (12)	196
Eve Grisenthwaite (13)	197
Victoria Westbrook (13)	198
Lindsey Haile (14)	199
Charlotte Baggott (14)	200
Jessica Rivers (14)	201
Roisin Richards (14)	202
James North (14)	203
Hannah Butterfield (14)	204
Nathan Longworth (13)	205
Lauren Phillips (13)	206
Joshua Lambert (13)	207
Lauren Kedward (12)	208
Georgina Lawrence (14)	209
Georgina Edgar (14)	210
Allegra Fowler-Wright (12)	211
Laura Jones (13)	212
Daniel Stamp (14)	213
Chris Davies (14)	214
Linda Bairkdar (14)	215
Jayne Sargent (12)	216

Sherwood Hall School & Sixth Form College, Mansfield

Matthew Appleby & Liam Commins	217
Amy Pearson (14)	218

Emma Louise Mayhew (13)	219
Heather Patton	220
Rachel Saunders	222
Jenny Patten (14)	223
Matthew Holt (14)	224
Victoria Winterton (13)	225
Emma Whitten	226
Shana White	227

South Wigston High School, Wigston

Edward Swingler (11)	228
Katherine Ardley (11)	229
Jessica Russell (11)	230
Rebecca Hemsley (11)	231
Charlotte Button (11)	232
Rebecca Norton (11)	233
Alice Dale (11)	234

Springwell Community School, Chesterfield

Daniel Bell (13)	235
Siobhan Kelly (12)	236
Abbi Carter (13)	238
Gemma Beach (13)	239
Skye Hopkinson (13)	240
Rebecca Bateman (13)	241
Natalie Lee (12)	242
Kelsey Stirling (13)	243
Jade Davies (13)	244
Heather Thomas (13)	245
Kerry McPhail (13)	246
Leigh-Marie Swan (13)	247
Jamie Barnett	248

The Garendon High School, Loughborough

Mariam Ahmed (13)	249
Helen Orr (13)	250
Hannah Bailey (13)	251
Rachel Blanchard (12)	252
Rachel Thorpe (13)	253
James Fairminer (13)	254
Edward Burdett (13)	255

Steven Bajor (13)	256
Neil Taylor (12)	257
Andrew Robinson (13)	258
Ethan Barnes (12)	259
Shelley Doyle (13)	260
Sophie Easton (13)	261
Kelly Bruce (13)	262
Leonie Amarasekara (12)	263
Beth Garton (13)	264
Naomi Warrington (13)	265
Annie Kirk (13)	266
Nikki Hoyle (12)	267
Mark Boyde-Shaw (13)	268
Sofie Bunce (13)	269
Alex Shephard (13)	270

The Phoenix School, Telford
Becki Mottershaw (12)	271
Sharese Pritchard (12)	272
Liam Clyne (11)	273

Woodhouse Middle School, Stoke-on-Trent
Melissa Hollies (12)	274
Sally Brown (11)	275
Natalie Yates (12)	276
Georgina Hollinshead (11)	278

The Creative Writing

Psychopath Returns!

We all thought he was a fictional character from the past and we all thought he had been slaughtered, but we were wrong.

The evil king, who became king by default, has now returned. Fresh evidence suggests Shakespeare's most famous character has come back to haunt Scotland - Macbeth!

We see Macbeth in films, but nobody knew he was a real being. Many directors have tried to copy the image of Shakespeare's description, but nobody has even slightly matched the description.

Scientist Andy Nam has discovered him. Just as Sir Shakespeare has described the illusory character, Macbeth's image has been caught on camera. He is described as a tall character, and with a stocky build. This new sighting could lead to many more discoveries of what we think of mythological characters.

Armed with a battle hatchet and a rapier in his satchel, Macbeth hacked his way through an ancient castle in Scotland. He has so far killed thirty-seven innocent civilians and the local police force has failed to capture this infuriated mortal. We are determined that this is not a common being dressed up. His face was translucent, and extremely pale in colour.

We are trying to trap the swine, but the television companies are not helping. They are hot on his trail and are trying to capture him on tape, but the scientist has declared this as impossible. He has formulated a precise chemical that has a neon radiance, which enhances the camera accuracy.

Anuj Patel (14)

Innocent

Gina was such a happy girl. Thirteen and her whole life before her.

It was February 2nd. Gina and her sister Melanie were strolling home from another joyful shopping day, carrier bags clutched in both hands. The sun started to set on the horizon and darkness began to fall. Melanie looked at the moon and said it looked lonely with no stars around it. Gina laughed. Smiling and joking they approached a road. The button to the traffic lights was pressed and they both waited patiently. They stood for a long time but no change was spotted in the lights.

Melanie sighed, 'Come on, let's go!' She ran halfway across the road when a bag accidentally fell out of her hands and fell on the floor.

'Mel, no!' Gina screamed. 'Mel!' she rotated and made a determined break for the lost items, then froze. A car came speeding her way, not stopping, not slowing down. Every second the car came closer and closer. Gina's heart threatened to burst through her ribcage with every beat. She and Mel had been friends since they were born. She couldn't imagine a day without her. Gina dropped her bags and violently shoved Melanie out of danger. The vehicle plunged into Gina's stomach. She fell to the road, her face covered in blood. Screams from Melanie splintered the night like a bandage torn from flesh.

Peering at the moon that night, Melanie noticed a star twinkling brightly. 'Thanks babe,' she said, smiling.

Adam Smith (13)
Beaumont Leys School, Leicester

The Day We Won The Championship

Amber's phone started ringing it was her mum, she was in Paris with Rachel's Mum. She said, 'We are doing a big design on Usher for his big photoshoot this evening, so I will be a bit late. See you later darling, bye!'

'Who was that, Amber?'

'Oh it was my mom saying that her and Rachel's mum are doing a big design on Usher.'

'Oh cool, phone her back and ask her to get some autographs for us,' said Kelly.

'She will anyway, she always does,' said Amber.

'Let's go and have a coffee and see if the radio is on so we can hear the football.'

Later on. 'I wonder if our dads have scored yet? Come on let's go in this one.'

It was second half and ten minutes into the game. Kelly's Dad had scored, it was 2-1 to them. Kelly was so excited, she couldn't wait until she got home to congratulate her dad.

They waited 20 minutes until it was over. They had won the championship 2005. They were so happy going home. They had a party for their dads, they had a really good time.

Rachel Cockram (12)
Belgrave High School, Tamworth

A Diamond Treasure

'Turn that music down girls, otherwise I'll turn it off altogether,' Rachel's mum shouted up the stairs, into Rachel's room.

'No, why should we?' Rachel answered back to her mum.

Vicky asked the girls if they wanted to go to the beach, the girls answered ... 'Yeah, why not!' Kelly replied. 'I mean, it's a nice day after all.'

'See ya later Mom,' screamed Rachel.

As the girls headed for the beach it started to rain, but it wasn't light rain, it was a storm!

'Hey, there's a cave over there, come on it looks dry!' said Kelly.

'But it's dark and ... and what if we can't find our way out of it!' replied Vicky, shaking like mad.

'Come on, you're not scared are you?' questioned Rachel.

'No, I'm just a bit worried that's all,' answered Vicky.

While the girls were still in the cave the rain got heavier and heavier.

'You two have you seen the rain? It's been raining for at least 2 hours,' complained Rachel.

'You two, look what I've found,' said Vicky.

'Is that what I think it is?' said Kelly.

'It's a diamond,' screamed Rachel.

'We've got to take it to the jewellers,' replied Kelly.

It had stopped raining by the time the girls had talked about the diamond. 'Come on, it will be closed by the time we get there, hurry up,' screamed Rachel.

As the girls reached the jewellers they couldn't wait to see how much it was worth. They ran inside the shop, Kelly asked a member of staff how much it would be worth. The girls were shocked when he said £21.6 million. The girls went home with £7.2 million each. They were very happy.

Victoria Simpson (12)
Belgrave High School, Tamworth

Lost!

This was the moment she'd been dreading. Ever since her friend Kelly's phone call two days earlier, Becky hadn't known how to be feeling about this day.

She was in town playing hide-and-seek through the shops with Kelly, Rachel and Charlotte, she'd got lost and she'd had no credit to ring anybody.

'I don't believe it! I knew this would happen. What am I going to do?'

Images flashed through Becky's head. Swirls of colour, one after the other. All of a sudden the 'Crazy Frog' tune raced through her head like a drum.

'H-hello?' she sniffled.

'Hi Bec, it's Rach! Where are ya? We've been looking everywhere.'

'Oh Rach, thank God it's you. I'm by, erm ... Argos. Can you come up and get me?'

'Alright then. See you in a minute.'

Sure enough, after what seemed like hours, the three friendly faces ran up to her.

'God Bec! We were really worried about you. How come you didn't come and find us?' Charlotte asked, slightly out of breath from all the running.

'Well, there's something I've kind of been keeping a secret from you guys. Um ... you might think I'm a bit stupid for this but ...' she stopped and looked at her feet, 'I've never been into town without my mum before so I don't really know my way round properly. That's why I didn't come and find you.' Becky breathed out heavily and waited for an answer.

'Oh come on Bec, don't worry! We're not bothered. Let's just go and enjoy ourselves.' The girls nodded in agreement and walked off arm in arm, laughing at what had just happened.

Kelly Day (12)
Belgrave High School, Tamworth

The Spooky Castle!

'Rachel, have you got our tickets?' shouted Ked.

'Yes, hold on a second,' Rachel replied.

'Quick you two, it's starting,' Charlotte said.

They all sat in front of the TV watching 'The Haunted Castle'.

'I hope we win,' mumbled Charlotte.

'Shush, they're about to read the codes out,' Ked said in a nasty way.

1st code. 'Yes, yes, I've won, yes!' Ked shouted happily.

2nd code. 'Yes, I've won, too, we are both going!' Rachel also shouted happily.

3rd code. 'I've won too, we are all going to the castle!' Charlotte also shouted happily.

They all danced around, thrilled they had won.

The next day they were all packing and met outside Rachel's house. When they all arrived they left for the bus. They slept on the bus because it was a six hour drive to the island where the castle was.

When they arrived at the castle they all started to unpack and get settled down in their rooms. After they had unpacked they got a chance to explore the castle. They wanted to see what it was like because none of them had ever stayed in a castle before and also they were only staying for the weekend.

The following day they got up and Charlotte said, 'Why don't we explore the island?' So Rachel and Ked agreed. They got changed and went exploring for a bit.

When they came back that evening they sat down and ate their dinner. 'I'm tired, I'm going to bed,' Rachel said yawning.

'Me too, I am going to bed as well,' Charlotte said.

So Ked agreed with them. After they had all finished their dinner they walked up the stairs and jumped into their beds and fell fast asleep.

The next morning they all got up grumpy because they had to leave at 5 o'clock. After they had eaten their breakfast they started to pack ready to go home the next day.

That evening Rachel heard a noise so she looked out the window and saw their bus so she shouted, 'You two, our bus is here!'

'OK Rachel,' they replied.

Charlotte grabbed the door handle and pulled the door, but it wouldn't open. Rachel took a step back and she heard a noise. Charlotte said, 'I'm scared, I want to go home.'

So they ran to the windows and they tried to open them, but they wouldn't open. So they tried the upstairs ones, they wouldn't open either. Then Ked saw a door above her so she opened it and they all walked up the stairs where they heard the voice again saying, *'Get out, leave at once!'*

The climbed out the window and jumped on the bus, the only thing any of them said was, 'Phew, I'm never going there again. That place is scary and *haunted!*'

Rebecca Scott (12)
Belgrave High School, Tamworth

To The Mission And Beyond!
(Inspired by Anthony Horowitz's books)

Roar! The rocket that Kaspar was in shot into the sky as fast as lightning. The engine was so loud that the two islands, ten miles away, could hear it. Nikolei Drevin was controlling it.

'Once my colleague places the bomb it will plough down into the Earth's atmosphere,' Nikolei sneered, 'and no one will know that I was involved in it!'

The professor of the rockets gasped. 'You can't be serious Mr Drevin,' Professor Chang explained. 'You've spent millions on building this hotel! Making it plummet into the Earth's atmosphere will be a waste.'

'Oh shut your mouth, you crackpot old fool. I'm the boss around here so go play with your chemistry set,' Nikolei Drevin replied. 'Or even better, *die!*' He pulled out a gun and shot Professor Chang in the brain. He became paralysed and collapsed to the ground.

Meanwhile, Alex Rider was using his judo moves to take out the last few guards on site. Once he'd done that he quickly sprinted towards the control site where the evil mastermind businessman Nikolei Drevin, was celebrating.

'Not so fast, Drevin!' exclaimed Alex. He had a score to settle with Drevin after he'd locked Alex up in an underground prison.

'You foolish boy,' Drevin chuckled, 'I've already launched Kaspar into space. In less than two hours, the Space Hotel will plummet into the ocean.'

'We'll just see about that,' Alex replied. 'In the meantime, I'll just fight you to the death.'

'Very well, let's duel!'

The fight was undoubtedly incredible. Fists were flying, kicks were hitting hard. It was as bad as a wrestling grudge match.

'You're a skilful fighter, Alex Rider, but no match for me,' Drevin smiled. He pulled out a gun and aimed it at Alex's heart. Alex looked round for something to block the shots and saw a knife that Drevin had dropped when he had killed Professor Chang. Drevin shot at him. Alex threw himself towards the knife, scooped it up and threw it at Drevin. The knife punctured Drevin's heart and he collapsed to the floor. Alex walked over to him to check if he was dead. No response. He was definitely dead. *The rocket,* he thought. Alex would never stop it in time. But then, after the panic attack, he noticed a button. He pressed it and felt good inside. Because on that button were two words *Self Destruct!*

Dominic Hookey (12)
Belgrave High School, Tamworth

A Birthday Treat To Remember

'Hi Amber, you know it's my birthday in a few weeks?' Kelly asked her in excitement.

'Yeah, how could I forget, you've been on at us for ages,' Amber replied.

'Well, guess what? My dad's taking me to Spain,' she told Amber jumping up and down.

'Cool, I wish my dad would take me to Spain for my birthday,' Amber complained.

'My dad said that I can take two friends and I've chosen you and Laura. We're going in a week's time, the 24th May. Wanna come?'

'That would be great, of course I do.'

After a long conversation, Amber, Kelly and Laura all met up at the local park to discuss their holiday.

A week later, the day had come for the girls to go on holiday for the first time without their parents, Kelly, her dad and Amber packed up the car and left for Laura's. They arrived at the airport to find out their flight had been delayed, but the good thing being it was only by an hour.

'Well, this is a good birthday isn't it, I'm glad it's not my actual birthday,' Kelly shouted as she sat down in the departure lounge.

'Well, it's not my fault darling. I'd fly that plane there if I could and you know that,' Martin (her dad) told her.

Eventually the plane arrived and all the luggage and people were loaded on. When they arrived at the hotel Kelly decided for her birthday that she wanted to go to the beach.

The next day they all woke up and sang 'Happy Birthday' to Kelly, gave her her presents and set off to the beach. Once they got there they lay their towels down and started to relax.

'Oh my life, that's hard, I'm moving,' Laura said grabbing her towel and bag and moving to the other side of Amber.

'What do you reckon it is?' Kelly asked wiping the sand swiftly across to one side.

'It's a box,' Kelly said picking it up out of the sand and opening it up.

'It's a watch, let's take it to your dad, he'll know what to do with it,' Amber said grabbing the watch and her towel.

The other girls grabbed their stuff and followed her down the road to where her dad was sitting. Her dad asked why they were back so early and the girls told him the problem. Martin told them to take it to the antiques person down the road. So they did. When they found it they asked the man how much it was worth and he said, 'That is a really rare pocket watch and worth around £5,000.'

'£5,000,' all the girls shouted.

'Well, this is a birthday to remember!' Kelly said.

Charlotte Stroud (12)
Belgrave High School, Tamworth

The Amazing Doll

In 1952 on the 24th May, it was Tillie's fifth birthday. Tillie is a kind, intelligent, shy girl with long, flowing, blonde hair and crystal-blue eyes. The clock struck 7. Tillie woke and jumped on her mum.

'Mum, Mum, where are my presents, where are they?' she shouted excitedly.

'Go downstairs and I will bring them down,' explained her mum, Jane. Jane was a generous and loving mother.

Opening all her presents with excitement, Tillie got down to the last one. She tore open the shiny pink wrapping paper and found a gorgeous doll, with long blonde hair like hers, a lovely baby-blue cotton dress with yellow squares and the most glistening green eyes you have ever seen. She loved it to bits, she played with it the whole day, it was the best present she had ever had.

That night she took it upstairs to bed with her. The clock struck 12. The doll awoke, stood up, strolled around Tillie's beautiful bedroom and finally after fifteen minutes she sat down. Then mumbled, 'This is better than that boring, mouldy shop window in which, when I'm awake, nobody is around.'

The doll next wrote a note, it read; 'To my owner, my name is Lulu and I am no trouble at all. All I need is a glass of milk and a couple of biscuits every night. Love from Lulu. PS Thank you'.

The clock struck 6, Lulu went to bed for another day. Tillie woke up and saw the note Lulu had written and decided to write one back. So she wrote, 'I got your note, thank you for telling me. I will bring your milk and biscuits every night. Love Tillie. PS Lulu is a lovely name'. Then she started to wonder when Lulu could have written the note and the only time she could think of was when she was asleep. So that night Tillie stayed up waiting for Lulu to wake.

Tillie was just about to fall asleep as the clock struck 12. Lulu soon awoke hoping to find more things about the house. She walked round the bathroom seeing what things did and then suddenly the light switched on, luckily she had just pulled the light switch by accident. Lulu carried on looking around the house. When she had finished upstairs, she crept downstairs into the living room. It was pitch-black and all the shadows looked like ghosts. Lulu was getting scared and started to panic. Her eyes were blurry. Her head hurt. She couldn't think straight. She was lifted up from the ground. It was Tillie. 'I thought you were asleep upstairs,' commented Lulu.

'Well you thought wrong,' answered Tillie.

'Well!'

'Sorry, it didn't mean to come out like that, so do all dolls come alive at night?' asked Tillie.

'No, and we do not come alive, we just sleep when you're awake.'

'What is that noise Tillie?' Jane shouted.

'Oh nothing, I'm just getting a glass of water,' replied Tillie.

'You have got to keep your voice down or else my mum will know,' Tillie told Lulu.

The clock struck 6 so they both went back upstairs to bed.

This happened many times after. They both loved having midnight feasts, telling stories, playing games and telling ghost stories. They did this every night at 12.

Laura Black (12)
Belgrave High School, Tamworth

Three Girls On The Scariest Holiday
(An extract)

'Wow! Look at everything! I never knew Florida was like this,' gasped Sarah looking out of the window in the hotel room.

'So what do you want to go and do first?' asked Alyx.

'Can we swim with the dolphins?' groaned Kirsty.

They had come to Florida for two weeks in the six week school holiday.

'Calm down! We need to tidy up first and anyway we've got two weeks!' exclaimed Sarah.

All of them went out for a wander round. Each of them took $40 with them.

'Do you like my new purse? My mom bought it for me,' asked Alyx. Her purse was light pink with dark pink stripes.

'Yeah, it's really nice,' replied Sarah.

'Ooo! Can we go in that clothes shop?' asked Kirsty excitedly.

'Yeah, OK, I need a new pair of jeans anyway, I've only brought six pairs with me,' replied Alyx, moaning.

Sarah bought two tops and one pair of jeans which cost $27. Kirsty bought an outfit which cost $20. Alyx was going to buy a top and two pairs of jeans. She went to the till, she put her hand inside the back pocket of her jeans and realised her purse was missing …

Kirsty Sands (11)
Belgrave High School, Tamworth

The New Kid On The Block

As I sat there, looking at what I had accomplished over the years. All my trophies sprayed out all over the shelves. Everything started to fade away. I shot up with a start to find out that I was only dreaming. It was race day today; it was mine and Michael Schumacher's first race of the new season. We had had a few pints the night before. We knew we shouldn't have, but thought it would be all right.

The phone rang, which gave me a start. I darted towards it. 'Room service, what would you like for breakfast?' said a jovial voice on the other end of the phone.

'Nothing thanks,' I replied.

Afterwards I got dressed and drove out to the track. I was all psyched up for the big race, if Michael or myself came first we would win. The excitement and the atmosphere around the track was tremendous. People and machines were buzzing around fixing things and souping up the engines for maximum speed when we were on the track. This was my first big race ever.

Ten minutes later, in my car and ready to go. First red ... then amber ... then *green!* The cars shot off from the starting grid reaching 60 going round the first corner. I reckoned that I was about third now. The adrenaline was pumping all around my body much like the fuel in the engine.

About an hour later, we were on the last lap, it was more or less a mad dash to the finish. I spotted ahead of me a car spin out and smash up his car, chancing a brief look at who it was. It was Michael. Therefore, I thought, *it is all up to me.* I reached the final bend, there was only one car ahead of me, so I thought, *what the hell!* I pressed the pedal hard to the floor, I was reaching 200; I could see the finish line. We were neck 'n' neck as we approached the line. Soon it was over. I had won! Was this the start of an illustrious career?

Ashleigh Williams (13)
Belgrave High School, Tamworth

The Volcano!

It was a peaceful day on the island of Crete and two boys were playing peacefully in the sand. 'This is boring,' Mark moaned. Mark, who was 14, loved volcanoes. 'Hey Graham, bet you won't be able to come to the volcano with me on Saturday?'

'Too right, I hate volcanoes!'

'Ha, ha! Too scared to go up a few little rocks. Go home and play with your Barbies!'

That night Graham thought about going up the volcano. His mind was so bend on it he couldn't sleep as he also remembered what Mark had said. It was playing on his mind like a broken record.

On Saturday Graham packed his stuff and went to Mark's house.
   'Hey come on then, we've got to get going, long time to go yet.'
   'What? You said you wouldn't come!'
   'I know, but I've changed my mind,' Graham said enthusiastically.
   Later that day they set off and by 5pm they were there.
   'Right, let's go.' Graham started to climb the sharp stone. Suddenly the volcano shook.

'What was that?' Mark whimpered, but still they climbed until they reached the top. 'Wow!' Mark said in shock.

Then it shook wildly! As Mark lost his footing and fell ...

'Mark!' Graham roared, but no reply. Feeling uneasy He started to climb down. Would he make it? By now he could see molten lava spewing rapidly out of the top of the volcano. Suddenly Graham felt a sudden sharp pain in his back and fell to the ground, knocked unconscious ...

Thomas Hughes (13)
Belgrave High School, Tamworth

The Sleepover

Yazmin, Ellie, Sasha and Crystal are the best of friends and go to the same school, Belgrave. All of the girls have different personalities.

Today was a great and exciting day. Ellie got back from holiday, (Spain). All of the girls were partnered together to do a project in history.

After school all of the girls went on a tremendous shopping trip. They brought expensive bright clothes and stuff for their project.

All of the girls slept over at Yazmin's house to do their project and have tremendous amount of fun. Sasha was like a pogo stick and couldn't keep still. Yazmin's house was a new mansion, full of fashionable things.

Tick-tock the clock was going, it was now 11 o'clock. The girls had finished their project and were having fun.

Crystal looked at the clock, it was now 3 in the morning. Yazmin was a parrot, the girls couldn't get her to shut up. Suddenly, all of the girls heard a groaning sound, it was coming from the basement. The girls crept downstairs. Yazmin and Sasha opened the basement door. Their faces turned white, they had just seen a headless ghost walk through Crystal.

They ran. Yazmin's mum and dad were out at a dinner party, so the girls were really scared. They were petrified and ran around the house like headless chickens.

Yazmin woke up, she was in her bedroom, the girls were asleep, it was just a dream.

Amy Williams (13)
Belgrave High School, Tamworth

The Haunted House

You could almost taste the smell of the old decay as the five of them slowly pushed open the steel door into a dark and gloomy passageway. You could sense the presence of something not quite real.

Lewis turned to his friends, he was a short, stocky lad and had a great sense of humour, but at that point nothing seemed funny. Ellie went first, followed by Dan and Lewis. Lee and Gemma crept slowly behind them staring at the walls which were covered in cobwebs.

As they tiptoed around, it felt like there were eyes everywhere, watching their every move. Lee wanted to go into the other rooms, the others didn't, but they reluctantly went. Lee stepped into the cold room. There was a thick blanket of brown dust that covered the whole house, but this room was different to all the rest, it was creepier and colder.

The house was like a museum, it was so quiet, all you could hear was Ellie crunching on her favourite strawberry lollipop.

Dan, the loudest of the group, started to feel even more uncomfortable saying how he thought they should turn back. 'You're not a baby are you?' whispered Lewis.

Dan closed his mouth, not wanting to be a coward and drifted along with Ellie.

Gemma had a strong feeling that something or someone was following them. Suddenly she saw a huge dark shadow towering over her. A stiff hand touched her shoulder, it sent a shivery chill down her spine. She then felt lifeless as if a vacuum had sucked everything out of her, she steadily turned around to see ...

Emma Rees (12)
Belgrave High School, Tamworth

Spooks Ville!

There lived two brothers named Paul and James. One day at school all of James' class was going on a trip to Spooks Ville, an old, odd village.

Paul wanted to go but his class wasn't going. So James decided that Paul could take a day off school, then sneak into the bus.

The next day Paul did manage to sneak into the bus and he went and sat at the back where nobody had been before. He sat at the back so the teachers would not see him. The back of the bus was dark, spooky and cold. James sat at the front of the bus next to Mr Hoot.

'At last,' shouted Paul. Paul came out the fire door on the left ... luckily James' class was on the right side so no teachers saw Paul.

Then a minute after, Paul found James. They both walked off. After thirty minutes Paul found an odd-looking house. It was small and fat. Paul fell to the floor, luckily James was still behind him and saved him. They both looked shocked because the house looked tall and thin inside, but outside it looked small and fat.

They both looked around the house and then saw some wood falling from the floor up above. A second later someone or something shouted, *'Get out!'*

James and Paul ran for their lives outside and told the others, but then Mr Hoot saw Paul and said, 'I'll speak to you at school!'

They all arrived at school and Paul told Mr Hoot everything.

Nathan Hill (11)
Belgrave High School, Tamworth

In The Mind Of A Victim
(Inspired by 'Invisible Mass of the Back Row!')

I stand in the middle of the classroom, surrounded by faces. The heat of the morning sun hitting me and making me sweat.

It's not long before that I start to tremble, while the eyes of the crowd stare at me. At the same time I feel a shiver go up my spine, like a spider crawling to reach the top of my spine. A few moments later, some people from the crowd start shouting comments to me. I want to stick up for myself and shout comments back, but words just won't come out - I feel like they have zipped my mouth together.

Gradually, my anger is building up inside of me, these rude comments aren't going to stop. It just feels like they all hate me. But what have I done?

Although I have stayed clear from people and stayed out of their business, they still seem to have an issue with me. They make me feel locked up and lonely.

Through the trauma, I hear lots of comments that are being shouted at me. 'Pathetic little girl, we don't like you!' I felt a tear run down from my eyes. Although, I feel upset and devastated - quickly wipe away the bitterness, just stop them seeing me cry. I just want to fall down and die. Make it stop please!

Kayleigh Williamson (14)
Biddulph High School, (Specialist Sports College) Stoke-on-Trent

Unknown

Why is it always me? I knew they were up to no good: my neighbours that is.

It all started on a cold winter's morning: the wind was howling like a pack of wolves and the trees' branches were like daggers ready to pounce on you at any moment. I woke up and the rain was like a herd of elephants passing by.

I heard someone coming; I guessed it was my dad, so I pretended to be asleep as I wanted to stay in my snug bed away from the cold. Unfortunately, it was my mum; she barged in and opened the window. 'That soon woke you up didn't it, now get up!' she snapped as she slammed the door behind her, leaving me with the bitter air that refrained me from getting up.

Then suddenly, there was a huge bang. I jumped out of my bed with fright. As I approached the window, I heard a voice shouting, 'Come on, move it!' I looked down and it was my loudmouthed neighbour ordering some men to carry gigantic boxes into the house. I began to feel very suspicious of my noisy neighbours.

Midnight came and music was booming next door. All that I remember is running into the road, then *bang!*

I am now lying in hospital recovering well, just wondering what happened that night. To me, it remains unknown.

Nathan Legg (15)
Biddulph High School, (Specialist Sports College) Stoke-on-Trent

Why The River Runs Red

In a village, deep in the heart of Africa lives a suffering community. There are very few old people in this village as many die young of famine and disease. Little food ever grows from the thirsty crops and little fresh water is supplied. The only source of water that has never been rationed is that of the murky river that flows past the dusty village. This river is a constant reminder to the people of the eternal torture they endure through their lives. The river serves as this reminder because the river runs a dark red, much like that of blood. Some people have said that the gruesome colour of the river is due to its muddy banks but the suffering people of the stricken village have their own theory. Whenever a newcomer asks why the river runs red they, the villagers, tell them the tale of the boy who created it.

A long time ago, the village was set next to a glorious whitewashed manor house. Separating the village and the house was a trench where long before men would dig for clay to make pottery. But now the clay had cracked from the hot sun and was no longer of use. The village had no source of water and the people would go days without a drink to quench their thirst. However, the elegant whitewashed house had a cobbled courtyard and set to the centre of the cobbled courtyard was a well of fresh cool water. The well tormented the villagers as they sat around possessed by the urging thirst that overwhelmed their cracking bodies. If anyone was caught trespassing on the forbidden land, that person would be hung.

The owner of the whitewashed manor was looking to employ a young boy to do odd things around the house; a young boy from the village offered his services and was gladly accepted. The boy was respectful and obedient to his master and would perform any task asked of him. His master took to the boy and decided to appoint more responsible jobs and the boy would be respectful and obedient to his master, although he hated him with passion for the suffering he chose to ignore. As the years passed, the owner of the whitewashed house grew fonder and fonder of his little worker and decided to award him anything he asked.

'You have performed great services to me my boy, I am grateful for this. So, I have decided to reward you with anything you ask for. Ask me for anything and you shall have it.'

The boy stood a strong posture for a moment, he was a careful thinker. He had grown tall and strong as his master had provided him with fresh food from the pantry and refreshing water from the well.

'I want you to provide a water supply for my people in the village. People die and grow ill every day; they need fresh water to drink and to soak the crops for food.'

His master looked at him for a time, stunned by the proposal. He had never interfered with the village past the trench as the people were dirty and poor; he wished not to lower himself. He had taken the boy in, he had saved him from the same grungy end and instead of being thankful, he asked to waste good water on the poor! The owner of the whitewashed house was infuriated and told the boy this in fruitful detail.

That night the boy snuck into his master's house and gagged his mouth so no one would hear the screams. After plunging a dagger through his master's heart he threw the bloodstained body into the well. The fresh water turned a dark bloody colour as the body of the boy's master bobbed on the surface like a blister. The boy broke through the wall of the well and the water gushed into the old clay trench.

The next morning the village people woke up to find the old cracked trench filled with water. The water was not clean and fresh but a bloody red colour. Some villagers wanted to drink it; but others did not as they believed the blood of the owner of the whitewashed house would be tainted with greed and arrogance. So they did not touch it and taught their children to do the same. As for the boy and the lifeless body of his master, they were never seen again.

As time has passed, little in the poor village has changed, including that of the tale of why the river runs red.

Stacey Bennett (15)
Biddulph High School, (Specialist Sports College) Stoke-on-Trent

The Missing Royal
(Inspired by the story, 'On The Sidewalk Bleeding')

How much longer will he take? It was starting to get dark and Laura was beginning to feel scared. She had been together with Andy for almost a year now and it was her 16th birthday.

Andy had decided to take Laura to a nightclub, where there he was planning on giving her his surprise gift, a diamond necklace. He had been gone for quite a while now and Laura was beginning to think he had just left her there.

It was streaming down with rain outside and Laura felt depressed and lonely. She had expected to celebrate her birthday having a thrilling time, instead she was stuck in the back of a smoky nightclub, all alone.

Minutes had passed, when suddenly a tall black-haired man came up to her and asked her if she cared to dance. Laura felt her cheeks glow, she had never been asked to dance with a stranger before. *Should I go for it or should I just sit and wait for a bit longer?* Reluctantly, she stood up, took his hands and made her way to the dance floor. *No one is going to ruin my birthday,* she thought once more.

Afterwards, when the clock struck midnight, Laura said her goodbyes to the friendly old gentleman that she had been dancing with for most of the night and she went to collect her coat.

She reached in her pocket and pulled out her phone and started dialling Andy, however, the only message that she received was the Orange answer machine with his sweet, soft voice. She longed to know where he was.

It was very late by now, so she decided to call for a taxi and make her way home. Although the only thoughts that ran through her mind were of Andy.

Where had he gone? Was he safe?

Katy Austin
Biddulph High School, (Specialist Sports College) Stoke-on-Trent

On The Side Street
(Inspired by the story, 'On The Sidewalk Bleeding')

Laura stood there, still. She couldn't speak or hardly move. She stood over his cold, lifeless body watching the blood dripping, flowing out of his side. All that she could think of was, *Andy, what happened? When did this occur? Could I have saved him if I'd come out earlier?* The policeman tried to talk to Laura, but her eyes were fixed on Andy's soaking wet purple jacket. She felt angry and annoyed whenever she looked at it. 'If he wasn't a Royal would he still be here, be here with me, not lying there dead?' she asked the policeman. At this point tears flooded her eyes, she wiped them away, although they kept coming back and soon she was in tears. Soon the ambulance came, the paramedics lifted Andy away. Laura got into the ambulance holding Andy's hand.

At the hospital, the nurses got in touch with Andy's parents. They came straight away. As soon as they came Laura went, she couldn't stand the waiting. She missed Andy. She stormed off going anywhere. She was not bothered about her life now.

She was now on the motorway walking across the bridge. She stopped, she watched the cars go past, watching, waiting, what could she do next? She thought her life was over. Although it wasn't, she felt like it had ended. All she had on her mind now was Andy. *What is he doing now? Where is he?* She always thought they'd die together, but Laura was wrong. Laura had a thought in her head.

If I jump off this bridge, me and Andy will be together. But if not I don't know how to deal with this. Laura got onto the bars, wondering what she should do next …

Jemma Goddard (14)
Biddulph High School, (Specialist Sports College) Stoke-on-Trent

Out Of Control

'Hit him, hit him,' they shouted.

Jan walked up to me and tried to hit me. I ducked and his fist strayed in mid-air. He tried to hit me again and, once again, missed. The crowd were becoming restless; in their bright green blazers, the sun reflecting into my eyes. I clenched my fist and threw it at Jan's face, catching his eye. Jan stood dazed for a minute, before lashing out and catching me on the chin with his strong, powerful fist. Then it happened. I went berserk, like a lion feasting on its prey. I just hit him. It felt like a thousand times. Then Mr Granger broke us up. Jan came out the worst, with two black eyes and a bust-up lip. He looked like a panda.

Jan was always giving me and other kids a hard time. It was the first time I had stuck up for myself. This was just a normal school day to me, except for the fight. All the picking on and name calling. Jan was in the same class as me and him and his friends always had their eye on me. Because I looked different, they treated me differently.

Finally it was science, last lesson of the day. I wasn't really paying attention, just daydreaming. Then Jan appeared.

'Me and you tonight at the park,' he said.

I just stared at his bruised face.

'What, are you chicken?' Jan shouted.

'No ... fine. Tonight at the park!' I replied in a shaky voice.

Matthew Rowan (13)
Biddulph High School, (Specialist Sports College) Stoke-on-Trent

Untitled
(Inspired by the story, 'On The Sidewalk Bleeding')

Why? Why did it have to happen to me? The feeling I had when I saw him lying there all alone, dripping with fresh blood. I was on my own believing that it was all my fault. Since that day I have quit smoking. If it wasn't for me he would still be alive.

See what happened was, I asked him to go and get me a packet of cigarettes, but he didn't come back. So I went looking for him I found him lying on the floor in a right state. At first I just thought he was so drunk that he had fallen asleep on the floor but no. I tried to lift him up but instead I felt blood leaking from his body onto my hand. I ran to find somebody who could help me. I spotted a police officer. When we got back to him there seemed to be no life in him at all. The police officer saw his jacket, he didn't look too impressed that he was a Royal. He took one close look at him then said, 'He's dead!'

He wrote something in his black notepad then radioed in that a dead Royal was in Fifth Street alleyway.

Five minutes later an ambulance turned up, put him in the back and drove away. There was no big investigation like on the television, they just took him away. I know why though. It was because he was a Royal.

Jonathan Bailey
Biddulph High School, (Specialist Sports College) Stoke-on-Trent

The Assignment

The four men and Santokh ran off down the path and on to the road. They ran a little, then started to walk. Sughra ran up the stairs to her father. She gave him the bag containing the noodles and then ran to the roof. She watched them cover a car with Kerosene oil and light it with oil torches. The car went up in flames. They stood and watched from the other side of the road. They then carried on walking down the street. I went back to my father. I started putting noodles on a plate for him, then I heard a loud bang - it startled me but I carried on dishing out the noodles.

For the next few months we struggled because my father was becoming more ill. We decided to risk fetching the local doctor, so we took a few friends to go and find him. We went to his clinic to see if he was there. He wasn't. We all panicked because we didn't know where he lived, we searched everywhere to find his details, but couldn't find any. We walked out disappointed with our heads down. I noticed a business card on the floor half covered in rubble. The other half slightly burnt. His house was only on the other side of town. But when we got there, the house was burnt down and covered in soot …

Aaron Hulme (14)
Biddulph High School, (Specialist Sports College) Stoke-on-Trent

The Sidewalk Bleeding
(Inspired by the story 'On The Sidewalk Bleeding)

I was dying because I was a Royal. Just a stupid bright purple silk jacket with big bold gold lettering saying *Royals*. I should have died because I was Andy, but no, it was just a jacket that caused my death.

I was thinking about what my mum and dad would say. I bet they would think I was a foolish boy. Then there is Laura. She is my girlfriend, my jacket was killing me and killing mine and Laura's relationship.

I was trying to shout for help but my voice just gave up. I felt the wound on my body and blood was pouring out just like pouring a teapot. A man came down the alley, he looked drunk but how would I know. He just said, 'Do you want another one? Well tough because it's all mine!'

Then a few minutes later, I felt a warm hand touch my wound. I knew it. But it was too late. She tried to lift my head but it just fell back. She knew it. I was dead.

A police officer came up to me and muttered, 'A Royal. Well better off without him.'

Chris Austin (14)
Biddulph High School, (Specialist Sports College) Stoke-on-Trent

The Dockside Rumble
(Inspired by the story 'On The Sidewalk Bleeding')

The rain was beating down on the docks. The smell of fish and the sound of the sea filled the air as the gang stood behind the pile of boxes as they waited for the signal. Then they heard the footsteps of the enemy, the group of adults and teenagers, each wearing the bright purple silk jacket of the Royals, stepped out from behind the boxes to see the other gang, wearing the dark blue jacket of the Guardians, then it started.

The Royals pulled out guns and knives from belts and the Guardians did the same, then they stood there, watching, waiting, waiting for the other gang to do something. The Royals started it with a gunshot and the Guardians retaliated with knives. The fight lasted for half an hour until the police arrived in helicopters with searchlights.

'Let's get out of here,' shouted one member as they retreated to shelter.

'Drop your weapons and step into the open,' shouted the loudspeaker. Some of the braver members fired at the helicopters but the bullets bounced off ineffectively. Again the voice ordered them to come out into the open like a master to his slaves. The members of both gangs retreated to hiding places. Police rounded up members of both gangs, but the Royals escaped. The Guardians would pay for the loss of Andy.

Jacob Chell (14)
Biddulph High School, (Specialist Sports College) Stoke-on-Trent

The Day That Changed My Life
(Inspired by Paragraph 1 of 'Deeper Than Colour' by Ijeoma Inyama)

Life never seems to change. Do *you* ever get that feeling when your life seems to have come to a standstill?

Mr Ratface, my form tutor, picks on me. It's so unfair. It's like the whole class are his little poisonous and infested 'ratlings' and I'm his adopted 'normal' child who is alone in a little corner suffering.

Even though I'm here now complaining about teachers and pupils, there is one plus about coming to this cardboard box in the sewers. Michael James. He's like the rat poison that clears all rats out of my vision.

Today, oblivious to me, things were different. Mr Ratface slacked off a little, his 'ratlings' didn't seem so poisonous and Michael James noticed me! I can't believe it. He came up to me and asked if I wanted to go to the movies on Friday night, of course I said yes!

Friday night soon came. Michael picked me up at 7pm. We walked as the movie was only a few blocks away. It was dark. As we walked down a dark alley, we felt a warm breeze. Michael's silky, smooth hair swayed gently, like grass on a summer's morning.

The alley seemed to darken further. Towards the centre of the path, a man's silhouette appeared in front of us. He was 6ft tall with a stubbled dirty face. He demanded money from Mike. Michael was determined to keep his money. I said he should give the drunken man what he had got. He refused as he insisted on taking me out.

I saw frantic movement from the arms, and it sounded as though there was a struggle, but I couldn't quite see. Michael told me to wait for him at the end of the alley, I didn't want to leave him but I felt as though if I could do one thing for him then this was it.

An hour later, Mike still hadn't come back to me. What had happened to him?

Georgina Wright (14)
Biddulph High School, (Specialist Sports College) Stoke-on-Trent

Where Is He Laura?
(Inspired by 'On The Sidewalk Bleeding')

'Where is he Laura?'

'He's gone to get some cigarettes.' Minutes passed. Laura thought nothing of it but when two hours had passed, she began to fret. *He's gone to the shop, he's gone to the shop!* Laura became panicky; calming her nerves by repeating frustrating thoughts that he didn't want to return, not that he couldn't return. She still feared for his safety, after all he was a Royal!

Laura decided to abandon the party, she walked down into the dark with the rain, drip, drip, dripping down her face. Turning down an alleyway, reaching the opening, she saw a man, just a man. A Guardian! Oh well just a Guardian! But no! in closer view she noticed a jacket on the floor. It was a Royal! She approached the man who was about a foot away from the jacket. It was him, him! Laura gasped a deep breath and then realised …

'No, not him! Not Andy!'

Hannah Shaw (14)
Biddulph High School, (Specialist Sports College) Stoke-on-Trent

My Last Thoughts!
(Inspired by the story 'On The Sidewalk Bleeding')

Why me? Why did I have to suffer? Oh yeah I'm a Royal! I'm an enemy, enemy of the Guardians but why me?

Royal, that's just a label, it's not who I am or what I am, I'm Andy, that's my name, that's who I am! Just because I'm in a gang called the Royals, it doesn't mean I'm bad! This is Andy, this is a Royal!

But what did Andy do? I know Andy, me, I didn't do anything to them, they did wrong to me! I'm Andy. Royal, that's not me! You have to look beyond the clothes to see who I really am! I'm Andy, I didn't do anything wrong.

I am not the one who does bad things, I am not the one who hurts people, I'm not the one! The person lying here isn't Andy, it's a Royal! It's unfair! Why me? It's not me who dying, it's a Royal! The last thing I heard was, 'That's for you Royal.'

Hannah Leese (14)
Biddulph High School, (Specialist Sports College) Stoke-on-Trent

Suicide

The exhaust fumes filled his lungs as he sat in the car. He would be dead in a matter of minutes and he would have none of the troubles that had affected him all his life. At this thought he smiled for the first time in a long time, as the world around him dimmed.

At that moment, an old couple walked down a country lane and found an unconscious man, face down on the steering wheel of a parked car. After calling 999, an ambulance carried the anonymous man to the hospital.

When he awoke in hospital, he found himself accompanied by his weeping mother. He hadn't thought about the effect his attempted suicide would have on the person he cared about most.

As the days passed, he spoke little and was very reserved when it came to confessing his problems to the psychiatrist, even so, he seemed to be getting better.

One day, on her way to visit him, his mother was in a fatal car accident. He now had no one to live for. This was the start of another downward spiral. When he got out of hospital, he checked into the nearest hotel.

The next day, when the cleaner opened the door to room 13, she was faced with a horrifying sight. In the middle of the room, a man was hanging from the ceiling, a leather belt around his neck. His life was over, his task complete.

Emily Wilkinson (14)
Countesthorpe College, Leicester

The Awakening

It was a dark, stormy night. The wind howled like a wolf and the trees creaked under its power. The moon was a ghostly galleon floating upon cloudy seas and the sky was blacker than darkness itself.

Down below was a horrific sight. Corpses lay scattered across a recently abandoned battlefield. Deep holes mauled the bodies and blood was still oozing from the deep wounds in the twisted corpses. Such was the great power of the Amphibians. A race of aliens, half amphibian and half humanoid, with technology surpassing that of all other races in the galaxy; all of which they had imprisoned. The last race to be enslaved was the Humans. However, upon enslaving this race a legacy awakened. An ancient power from the times long forgotten by most humans. This terror was prophesied by an Amphibian psychic. This power would tear through their armies, feeding on the strength of the warriors, before annihilating the commander general and dispersing the control that they had. This terror was known as the vampires. A race that moved on the wind, through the darkness and struck with the power of an entire nation. It was then that they attacked and ripped through the Amphibian armies annihilating every warrior in seconds. The general stood face to face with the first and most powerful; Dragounis. In one swift movement Dragounis ripped the general's head off and freed the imprisoned races, before returning to his sleep; to wait until he was needed again.

Darren Wallis (14)
Countesthorpe College, Leicester

Quest's End

The man stood in the dawn light, outline blurred by the fire encasing his cloak, billowing out behind him as he stared at his goal. Dark eyes narrowed to penetrate the murky gloom that surrounded the keep. Comrades surrounded him as they set up the Legionnaire.

A simple gesture of his steel-plated hand and the Legionnaire opened fire. Two plasma cylinders attached to the main triangular body released their deadly cargo. The power was released from the Crystal atop the Legionnaire. It glowed sickly green before the beam sped into the keep. The gothic stonework buckled and ran like mercury under the onslaught while the men on top disintegrated into their component atoms. A crater, twenty metres in diameter, appeared where the energy discharge stopped.

The man smiled as he gripped his jewel-encrusted broadsword and led the rest of his group into the breach. The remaining soldiers on the walls jumped down to confront the intruders. They mobbed the man with the blazing cape but could not stop him with their axes. He had a glittering web around him where no man could live as he swung his sword with the grace only a First had on a planet like this. His anger transformed itself into pure heat burning any flammable object, like his cloak, around him. He swept through the defenders and into the hall. There, in the alcove was his prize, the soul catcher interface. He raised his sword and roared his victory over the Carack-Tar.

Sean Creasey (14)
Countesthorpe College, Leicester

Untitled

It was pouring down with rain. Thunder and lightning were striking the trees. The horse galloped through the wet, slippery mud. The horse slipped and went rolling down the embankment into a pile of dead leaves and wood. I fell and landed on sharp, cold rocks. I could feel myself choke in my armour as the water rushed through the gaps in the helmet. I could hardly breath. The armour weighed down on my cold body. I felt I was going to die.

Suddenly I could hear a horse galloping through the water, it stopped dead and my helmet was wrenched off. The cold rain fiercely hit my face. I looked up and there it was - staring back at me, eye to eye.

Philip Nicholson (15)
Countesthorpe College, Leicester

After School With Grandma

I could hear the old-fashioned music as I stood in the porch, my school bag felt heavy on my shoulders. Did my mum and dad realise as they sat at work, that every day after school, they leave me with a little old woman who can barely take care of herself, never mind me? I took a deep breath and nervously gave the rusty doorbell a poke. Awaiting the very same sentence, I heard this line every day. The door opened with a creak, "Ello darlin', give yer old grandma a kiss. Avent yer grown since the last I saw yer?'

I seriously doubted if I had grown since yesterday, I put my things in the cupboard and sat myself in the living room. The room would be quite big if it wasn't filled with pointless clutter, like stuffed dead animals in glass cases and cardboard boxes filled with tacky ornaments and old toys. Nothing in the room matched, there were two armchairs, one was red made with a velvet-like material, the other had green and white stripes. I switched on the TV, the picture was black and white and the sound was of poor quality, it kept making an annoying scratching sound.

Mum might be back soon, I couldn't bear any more stories about, 'Back in my day,' 'Dorothy from bingo,' or her bald cat Mr Sniffles. (Not a true story!)

Sam Hirst (14)
Countesthorpe College, Leicester

A Day In The Life Of A Horse

The sun's rays covered a field of daisies and the warmth brought out more wild flowers. I galloped past a large oak tree and the breeze flowed through my white, clean mane. The whistling of my owner commanded me to gallop around the field and back to my owner. It was time for a hack out. She guided me to the stables with my head collar and tacked me up with my saddle and reins. I obeyed her, I loved hacking out along the roadside and through the fords.

We walked out and onto the side of the road. I was excited to be going out so I had to be calmed down. A red car drove past us on a corner. Another car appeared on the other side causing the overtaking car to swerve. The horror of the car coming towards me and my owner was so frightening, I was startled and I reared up.

My owner fell off me and the car came hurtling into the ditch behind us. My owner was lying on the floor and someone from another car called an ambulance. Within no time an ambulance arrived and the people from the car and my owner were removed from the vehicle and into the ambulance. A stranger took me back to the stables. I struggled and played up as I was shocked and panicking. I was released back into my field and I walked slowly to the oak tree. I laid down in the shade watching the red sun set.

Carly Dolman (15)
Countesthorpe College, Leicester

Short Story

A van pulled up outside the town shop and parked normally between the parking lines. The engine turned off like any normal van, however, no one got out.

'This doesn't feel right.'

'Don't worry just do the same as last time.' Then two men dressed all in black with masks on jumped out, sliding the van's doors open.

One was holding a large, deep bag, the other with a small gun. they both ran in, one pointing his gun at the shopkeeper, while the other stood between the counter and the door, holding the bag wide open. The man with the gun shouted, 'Empty the money into the bag.' The other man walked nervously towards the counter, holding the bag over the counter.

The shopkeeper opened the till slowly and reached down to get the money, noticing the red police button under the counter. He slowly pressed the button, before reaching in to get the money from the till. There were only a few coins and notes but he still placed it all in the bag.

'Is that all?'

Suddenly a man who must have overheard in one of the other aisles, leapt out shouting.

The man with the gun jumped in his nerves, shooting the shopkeeper in the shoulder by accident. The keeper fell to the floor. The other one dropped the bag, shouting, 'This is murder.'

'Get out, quick!' the other man called, while dropping his gun to the floor. They then ran out the shop jumping into the van like two normal robbers.

Alex Marvin (15)
Countesthorpe College, Leicester

A Day In The Life Of Bert The Snail

I woke up suddenly to find it was pouring down with rain. I don't like rain, it washes away my slime trails that I spend ages making.

My morning was boring, I spent it travelling across the moist grass to the other side of the garden. The rain splashed down on my shell as I arrived at the Sycamore Tree restaurant for a meal with my old friend Boris. We had a really nice meal, I had a wet leaf and Boris had a piece of sycamore stem.

We left at about 2pm and went our separate ways. I wandered off to the nearby Bush Hotel for a while, while I had my afternoon nap. I was wrapped up in a nice leaf until unexpectedly I was disturbed by a giant hand picking me up out of my comfortable leaf, into the cold and wet air. It was a stupid young boy. He sat me in the palm of his hand and stared at me. He had bright ginger hair and lots of freckles. I rolled up into my shell to avoid looking at him any longer.

I can't remember what happened next, all I know is that I suddenly felt like I was flying. I came round and found myself in a completely different place, it was dark and much bigger than normal. The kid had obviously thrown me over the fence.

Ah well, this garden looks nice and comfy. I will explore it tomorrow but for now I need to sleep.

Steven Richards (14)
Countesthorpe College, Leicester

AC Milan Vs Liverpool

Shevchenko 'I am very disappointed ...'
Interviewer 'I guess you are very upset with tonight's slumbering of Liverpool 5-2.'
Shevchenko 'Well yes of course I am very upset, when we were up 2-0 at half-time then go and lose!'
Interviewer 'You got one of the goals and it was quite a cracker!'
Shevchenko 'Yes it was, I pulled it and got the prize, that's the only good thing that came from the night!'
Interviewer 'I bet you were in dreamland at half-time weren't you?'
Shevchenko 'We were until the 75th minute, then we just got tired and couldn't carry on!'
Interviewer 'Well thank you for talking to me and good luck for next season!'
Shevchenko 'Thank you.'

Now let's talk to Liverpool captain Steven Gerrard ...

Interviewer 'Hello Steven, congratulations!'
Gerrard 'Thank you.'
Interviewer 'You got Liverpool's first goal and that was the goal that bought them back into the game.'
Gerrard 'Yes, straight into the second half, great pass by Alonso and, as you said it, bought us back in it.'
Interviewer 'I bet you thought it was all over in the dressing room at half-time?'
Gerrard 'Well yeah, we did but I still had a glimmer of hope.'
Interviewer 'Are you going to sign a new contract?'
Gerrard 'Yes I will be talking to Rafa as soon as I can.'
Interviewer 'Well good and congratulations again and thank you for talking to me.'
Gerrard 'Thank you, bye.'

Now let's talk to match-winning manager Mr Rafael Benitez

Interviewer 'Well debut season, great success, one trophy, two finals. Congratulations.'
Benitez 'Well thank you, I think we deserved that a lot.'
Interviewer 'You definitely did. How do you think your team performed tonight?'
Benitez 'Very, very, very well from the 45th minute to the 90th we played like we have never played before.'
Interviewer 'Well Djibril Cisse, amazing isn't he?'

Benitez	'Yes he is brilliant, came on in the 75th minute and ended up with his name on the score sheet three times.
Interviewer	'Well thank you for speaking to us.'
Benitez	'It's OK!'

Now finally we'll speak to hat-trick hero Djibril Cisse

Interviewer	'Hello Djibril, very, very many congratulations. Where shall we start on the win or the hat-trick?'
Cisse	'Well thank you, I am very happy, this is the best day of my life.'
Interviewer	'You only came on in the 75th minute and somehow got a hat-trick.'
Cisse	'Well yes, it was my first Liverpool hat-trick and it came at the right time.'
Interviewer	'Yes it did, well congratulations and good luck in the near future at Liverpool football club and we can't wait to be seeing you again next season.'
Cisse	'Thank you, bye.'

Mitchell Wickes (12)
Elliott Durham School, Nottingham

Best Friends!

It is the first day back at school and the four friends are in the playground talking about a new girl that is starting this term.

'Hey, have you girls heard? There is supposed to be a new girl starting,' Rusheba said.

'Yeah, do you know if she is nice and kind? Do you want to be friends with her?' Kayleigh suggested.

'Alright,' the rest of the girls answered.

They were now in their classroom working really hard when there was a knock at the door. The head teacher came in with the new girl.

'Good morning, now this is Chloe, she is new here and I expect you to make her feel welcome. That is all, goodbye,' the head teacher said.

'Chloe, you can go sit next to Lindsey,' Miss whispered.

It was now break time and the four friends were talking about Chloe.

'Chloe seems alright. Let's ask her to be our friend,' Samantha said.

'Yeah, but she is friends with Lindsey, we will have to break them up 'cause Chloe has made a big mistake,' Shelley exclaimed.

'I know 'cause her and her three friends are really mean and think they rule the school when they do not,' Samantha remarked.

'I know I nearly did the same thing when I started here. I mean they think people respect them when they are just abominable,' Rusheba said.

Chloe and Lindsey and Lindsey's other friends were sitting on the bench talking about their friendship.

'I think we are going to be best friends forever,' Lindsey exclaimed.

'Wait, I do not want to be friends with you! Sorry Lindsey, bye,' Chloe said. Then she slowly walked towards Kayleigh and her friends.

'Excuse me but I like you a lot, can I be friends with you please?' Chloe asked.

They looked at each other and smiled.

'Yeah, OK you can be our friend, you seem like a very nice person. Do you want to meet up at the Sugar Ball to celebrate? First drinks are on me!' Kayleigh said.

'Alright but the second round is on me,' Chloe said.

They were friends forever.

Sarah Lee (13)
Elliott Durham School, Nottingham

A Day In The Life Of Bart Simpson

I wake every school day at 7.30, switch the alarm clock off but don't get up, I wait till Mum comes in (at the last minute) and then pretend to feel sick (it sometimes works) but normally she sees right through me. When I finally get downstairs I have Krusty cornflakes then Lisa complains that she is going to be late and miss maths or something (isn't maths horrible). When I get to school I try a little fake heart attack (just as a last resort) and slowly plod into school.

In lessons I am always a *good boy* putting my hand up for every question but there's a hitch, I answer them wrong! Like this one, teacher says, 'What is the capital of France?' and I say, 'F Miss!' Then everyone laughs (I love attention). One of my favourites is making rude noises, it is a hobby of mine (no lesson is complete without rude noises).

At dinner I am always first in line ordering the healthy option - potatoes, carrots, peas and meat. I wait till Nelson (school bully) sits down then I start throwing mashed potato at him (he has started expecting it now) of course we get sent to Skinner's office (the principal) but I don't care it is always worth it.

When I go home I zoom back on my skateboard, but on the way I change signs around, an example would be changing the *Bus Stop* and the *Don't Park Here* signs.

Finally at home I put my feet up and watch TV then go and annoy Lisa by changing her maths book and her English book around so she does algebra in English and writes a letter in the maths. And lastly, just refuse to go to bed.

Elizabeth Taylor (12)
Hope Valley College, Hope Valley

A Day In The Life Of The Queen

I wake every morning at about nine o'clock and call for my ladies-in-waiting to help me get dressed and washed and help me go down so I can eat breakfast. Then I read all the letters from people and write my speeches.

I have four houses, one that I live in that is called Buckingham Palace and another one that I sometimes live in that is called Windsor Castle. The two other ones are called Sandringham and Balmoral where I go on my holidays. My favourite place is Balmoral because it is in Scotland and I like to see Prince Philip in a kilt.

I am a kind and generous person, I like to help people when they are stuck. I'm lucky enough to visit a lot of places around the world. I also speak a few words in certain foreign languages when I visit other countries. My favourite places to visit are the Commonwealth countries.

I live with my husband Prince Philip, a lot of servants and my seven dogs who are all corgis. My seven dogs' names are Dolly, Daisy, Shandy, Molly, Blacky, Brandy and Candy. I also go and see my children - Prince Charles, Princess Anne, Prince Andrew and Prince Edward.

My hobbies are horse riding and walking my seven dogs.

Sophie Kellett (12)
Hope Valley College, Hope Valley

A Day In The Life Of Jaws

Hi I'm Jaws. I live in the sea around Australia because I can snack on all the surfers. I tried living in the USA but the Americans taste too fatty. Anyway as I was saying, I live in Australia.

I wake at 8am every morning because that's when the fishermen go fishing (you know they taste very good with a bit of seaweed). When breakfast is over I swim around nipping people's legs. It's only a joke but they seem to take it seriously and everyone jumps out of the sea. I love this because I can swim round with people shrieking and pointing at me. At around 1pm I have lunch. This consists of 1 small child lightly tanned, 2 surfers, sunburnt and 1 woman, very pale (yum).

By this time the whole beach is deserted so I swim round the coast to the south beach and play a little game, where I see how many times I can bite somebody before they notice.

For tea I have 2 dolphins. Stupid dolphins, they think they are so cute, I mean have you ever heard of a shark being called cute?

I must go now, bye.

Hannah Stanish (12)
Hope Valley College, Hope Valley

A Day In The Life Of The Queen

I wake every day at 9am and read a chapter of a book - usually a classic like 'Jane Eyre'. My waiter brings me breakfast at 9.30. Breakfast is usually two Weetabix with a teaspoon of sugar, skimmed milk and a glass of orange on the side. My corgis always come on the bed in the mornings. My cleaner gets annoyed because she has to wash the bed sheets twice a day because they are covered in dog hairs.

I am usually dressed at about 10am and then I go for a stroll around the gardens, as this is my daily exercise. I love it in May to June time because all the flowers are out and the sun is shining. I walk for approximately 2 hours and then I go in for lunch. Lunch is usually seafood and salad. I love the taste of mussels, but they are so much better if they have just been caught.

At 1pm Tony Blair calls in for a chat. He usually stays for afternoon tea, which is at 4pm. He leaves as soon as the scones are gone.

At 5pm all the royal family come for dinner, which is a roast. I go to bed at 9pm because I need the sleep.

Anne-Marie Higgins (12)
Hope Valley College, Hope Valley

A Day In The Life Of Bart Simpson

Hi, I'm Bart Simpson the famous cartoon character. I am 10 and I live in 73 Evergreen Terrace in Springfield. I live with Homer, Marge, Lisa (idiot) and Maggie. My favourite catchphrase has to be, 'Eat my shorts' and I would like to fulfil my dream and eat my shorts one day.

Every day my Krusty alarm clock wakes me up at 7am I pretend to be ill but Mum knows me too well. I pull on my blue shorts and orange top and charge downstairs. I eat my breakfast of Krusty-Os, I love Krusty-Os. Lisa doesn't but she's a girl and girls are weird.

I pack my bag with all the school essentials, cherry bombs and maps to the teachers' houses. I run back upstairs. Homer is there trying to get to work on time. He never makes it though and he won't today. Mum grabs me and tries to comb my 9 spikes flat but I wriggle free.

I miss the bus as usual and Mum refuses to give me a lift so I end up walking - skateboarding the 4 blocks to school.

When I get to school I realise I haven't done my homework. I never do and I don't care because all they can do is give me a detention. I'll have to write something stupid on the blackboard like, *I will do my homework*.

I have to say, school is for geeks and I am most certainly not a geek. Lisa is a geek she loves school but as I said she's a girl and girls are weird. I am always so glad when school is over. No more Skinner or Krabappel. I will normally catch the bus this time after my detention.

When I get home Mum will be cooking tea, Homer will be on the couch with a Duff and the football on the telly and Lisa will be revising. On Friday (today) it's pork chop night. Mum will want us to chat about our day but we never do. Lisa doesn't eat pork chops because she's a vegetarian.

I would like to stay up all night and I would if it was up to me but it's not. Mum says I have to go to bed at 8. I try and fight back but Mum always wins. Bed it is.

Sarah Jenkins (12)
Hope Valley College, Hope Valley

A Day In The Life Of The Queen

One wakes at 7 o'clock in the morning, on most weekends one wakes at 8 o'clock but if one's got plans for the day, one still wakes at 7.

One likes a simple breakfast, maybe slightly scrambled egg with dry cured bacon, grilled tomatoes and mushrooms. On weekdays one likes to lounge on the balcony with Richard (a 17-month-old corgi), whilst eating one's breakfast.

Most weekends, one likes to go horse riding with Charles. Meanwhile, Harry and William go clay pigeon shooting behind the stables. They always come home arguing over who is the better shot. Sometimes Charles and I may finish our riding early, so we wander round the stables meeting the grooms as they tend to their horses' needs.

In the evening, one prefers to stay at the palace but that isn't always the case. One may have to give a speech to the National Health Service or the NSPCC.

For dinner, Fredrick prepares delicious and extravagant dishes, such as purée of parsnip soup or smoked mackerel pâté for starters. He prepares crown roast of lamb with lemon or paprika beef with garlic and clove for the main course. He can make such wonderful desserts as iced strawberry soufflé and tipsy fruit compote with cinnamon.

One likes to finish one's day with a nice hot bath with essences of camomile or lavender. One prefers to retire at 10 o'clock as tomorrow plans for the day have been made.

Tom Jolley (12)
Hope Valley College, Hope Valley

A Day In The Life Of A Bully

I wake up with the sound of my alarm clock ringing in my ear at 7am. Then I get dressed and eat my breakfast. I can her my mum in the shower. Brilliant, now's my chance to nick some cigarettes from my mum's handbag.

On the way to school I meet my mates at the corner shop, then we make our way to school.

For dinner I eat chips and beans, as well as a Year 3's packed lunch. Then I'm off to the playground. Me and the leader of our gang, (Jonny) go and corner some little kids until Miss Hanly comes out and sees us.

It's 4.30pm, the end of school. I start to walk home. Jonny taps me on my shoulder and asks me if I want a cigarette and of course I've got to say yes. It's so awful when I inhale the smoke, it makes me want to throw up but I don't tell or show that to my mates.

I get home and my mum's got my tea on the table for me which is good as usually she's at work. I watch telly for about 2 hours until my Mum shouts for me to go to bed. Then I go to sleep, hoping my mum won't tell me to go downstairs and clean the mess of chocolate bar wrappers I left.

Vanessa Morgan (12)
Hope Valley College, Hope Valley

A Day In The Life Of John Terry

I wake at 7am usually because of my son but that's not the reason for today it's because I have a football match. It's England against Brazil. I bet you can guess who I play for. I was born in London.

So I go downstairs and have a bowl of muesli, it's really healthy for you. After that I go and have a shower. Also I need to get dressed so I go upstairs to my wardrobe and there it is, my most prized possession, my England kit. I get it on and go back downstairs, looking at the chandeliers.

I go to the door and my butler opens it for me. I stare at my Porsche and go over to it and get in tiredly as it is only 9am and drive to the Old Trafford stadium.

When I get there it is 11.30, only half an hour till kick off so the team starts doing stretches and warming up. Then Sven (our manager) calls us over for a team talk. He tells us what to do.

We get in our places and kick off. Nothing happens until the 23rd minute, Ronaldo runs up and shoots from 20 yards out. It goes straight past our goalkeeper. We are 1-0 down, we keep on trying but can't get a goal in the first half.

We then kick off the second half. It is the 50th minute and Rooney gets brought down in the penalty box and we get a penalty. Owen takes it and places it perfectly in the back of the net. It is now 1-1. We have kept our hopes up tried our best and it is now the 90th minute. We get a corner. I go up, Beckham takes it and I head it in the back of the net. The crowd go wild. It is now 2-1 to England.

The full-time whistle goes and we've won the cup. The team are so pleased. We all go home and when I get home I am so tired I have a quick nap.

Jack Langley (11)
Hope Valley College, Hope Valley

A Day In The Life Of Donkey

Usually I wake up at eight o'clock, an' if you think that's late, you should see ma uncle Jaspa he gets up at eleven o'clock every mornin', speakin' of which, tomorrow mornin' I'm makin' waffles. Shrek says he won't let me. I'll have to eat what he eats if I'm gonna lodge wi' him. But his diet is disgustin' an' I don't dare repeat what he keeps in his bedroom.

After ma pretty normal breakfast of toast an' jam, I follow Shrek around, partly to annoy him (I have a knack for dat), an' partly to have a bodyguard. Havin' an ogre around isn't all that bad when you think about that part of it though. There are some strange creatures in the swamp that wouldn't dare come near me if I had Shrek wi' me. I cannot deny havin' one dull moment wi' Shrek though, every day he intends to do something dull, but I object to that an' off we go kickin' Lord Farquaad an' his army's asses. After dat we head off for Shrek's humble home (sarky). We usually miss lunch so ma supper usually consists of cheese on toast (as you've guessed I do like ma toast). After dat I go outside to sleep it all off an' be ready to do something else another day.

Rachel Taylor (12)
Hope Valley College, Hope Valley

A Day In The Life Of Shrek

I awake from my heavy burden of slumber. My throat has apparently committed suicide ... again. I realise that one too many oiled slugs are not great for one's gullet. They can be a gigantic toil if you're not too careful. Oh who am I kidding, playing the posh aristocrat? I'm gonna start again.

I open my eyes to the sound of birds calling from their nest, within reach of the window. Five minutes later, I have breakfast in bed, thrushes' eggs fried well - and also a roast thrush. To wash down, dried, liquidised, cancerous rat, obviously dead by the drying and the liquefying and the cancer and all. This takes a couple of seconds depending on how much boiled log I've had the previous night. One or two belches and the meat is done. This is a typical start to the day.

I get ou' bed, an' 'url meself at the sewage system. I 'ave a sludge shower, pullin' the chain as 'ard as it can go if it's not already broken ... I run out and dive at the huge pond, where my daily morning fart will occur. This will take the lives of about three fish on a good day, on a bad day ... grrrr ... I'm speakin' posh 'gain! My personal best is five, but I've 'eard of an ogre making eleven, bu' tha's just impossible.

I brush my teeth with anything that comes into contact with my hand, be it a rock or a plain dead old fish - deceased by a fart. I will usually lie down for a nap until lunch or maybe that stupid donkey will turn up. He always insists on going on an 'adventure'. I reply by saying, 'I'll give you an adventure you'll never forget.' The next half hour is too explicit to put words to, even publish for that matter. Ohh - if you really want to know I'll tell you. For Donkey the consequences will be several nasal injuries, an extra hard 'massage' and a good ol' kick up the backside! For me ... a jolly good time!

Lunch is small but satisfying. Merely being a sawdust sandwich (that's the small part). I'll usually tempt Donkey to get the sandwich and run round 'til he runs out of breath (that's the satisfying part). I will usually fall to the floor laughing, falling asleep, until I will make myself a huge dinner, always including an assorted arrangement of oiled slugs, each of a very good vintage. My liver by now is past its best, unlike some of my bottles! They are amazing, each one coming all the way from ... errr ... about twenty-six feet away from the front door.

Earwax is pulled from the ears, creating a magnificent candle. A rat's tail is then placed in it, as a wick.

The average time it takes to eat is twelve hours, considering I eat myself into the next day and then the same happens for the next year, then my patterns are randomised and I shall eat rice for a week. Such is life with me.

Rory Loveless (12)
Hope Valley College, Hope Valley

A Day In The Life Of Shrek

Hi my name is Shrek and I live on my own in a swamp. I love it on my own, well from what I can remember.

I was just sitting down for a nice meal of bug burgers when I heard scuttling coming from outside. At first I thought it was my friend Donkey but then I went out to tell Donkey to shut up and was surprised at what I saw. Hundreds of fairy-tale creatures crowded round my swamp. Furious, I demanded someone tell me what they were doing there. One of the seven dwarves told me everything. Lord Farquaad had sent them.

I hurried to his kingdom to get my swamp back. I ended up in a big fight and got sent to find some princess to marry Lord Farquaad.

Now I'm on a big journey with an annoying donkey humming all the way. Great.

Katie Brierley (12)
Hope Valley College, Hope Valley

Myth

A long, long time ago in a small village there was trouble. Past the cold mountains, past the waterfall and its rickety bridge, deep in the woods of the dead was this small village where all the damned were to live for eternity. Only one man there was holy, he had been sentenced for a crime he did not commit. What this crime was, nobody knew. They say the court vanished. His name was Dovile.

In the centre of this village was a well and every day Dovile would warn the people of the danger that lay below. 'It is the porthole to Hell, I tell you!' he would try with all his might but his attempts fell on deaf ears. They would call him cuckoo, crazy and bonkers.

One night in the cold, dark air a shadow poured out of the well. It crept round each hut, killing any children in sight and painting their bedrooms with goats' blood. A sea of blood coated the huts.

In the morning many villagers were gathered round the evil well, looking for its demon. They rattled pitchforks and desperately screamed down the well until a force pulled them down. They fell and screams echoed and burst out of the well.

During that night every woman was killed. A committee of knights decided enough was enough. They tossed fire and everything they could down the well. A swift wind blew away the flesh of the knights and their bones and armour collapsed on the floor.

They say after that there was no one left, but there was. Dovile put a wooden lid on the well and ran past the waterfall and over its rickety bridge, up the cold mountains, speaking gently to himself, 'It's the porthole to Hell. I told you!'

What happened to Dovile after that I do no know, some say he perished in the cold, others say he is still there but I reckon he is travelling to the far corners of the Earth, warning people about the Devil and trying desperately to save lives.

Richard Achahboun (12)
Hope Valley College, Hope Valley

A Day In The Life Of Shrek
(An extract)

My name is Shrek, and I'm different to other people, you see I'm an ogre. I live in my own swamp. I like my privacy, and I like my space, so I have signs, saying *Keep Out,* and pictures on of me, but much scarier.

I usually wake up at 9am. At weekends, I lie in. I have a mud bath. After that, I go into my lake to relax, oh and my morning fart, gotta have my morning fart or I get wind through the day (smelly)!

I usually have breakfast at 9.30 or 10, depends. My breakfast is crusty slugs with insects insides. Actually that's what I always eat.

Some days I renew my signs, and today is one of those days. I'm putting up my signs and I can see something glittering. It's a poster, and it says, *'Wanted - Fairy-tale Creatures - Reward'.*

Now I can hear something just over the hill. It sounds like people are shouting, 'Fairy-tale creatures wanted'. It must be something to do with the poster I picked up earlier. I think I heard somebody just say, 'My donkey can talk.' I'm thinking, *a donkey talking? Yeah, whatever.* All of a sudden it sounded like a man hissed. 'That will be good for 10 shillings, if you can prove it,' or something like that. The argument went on and on and the man got so annoyed and shouted, 'Guards! Take her away.' It sounds like the lady kicked something over and hit someone. All of a sudden, somebody shouted, 'I can fly.' Someone else shouted, 'He can fly!' Somebody else wailed, 'He can fly!' The man shouted, 'He can talk.'

The donkey said, in amazement, 'Oh that's right, I'm a flying, talking donkey. You may have seen a house fly, maybe even a super fly, but I bet you've never seen a donkey fly!'

A couple of seconds later there was a thud, and somebody shouted, 'Seize him!' You could hear running, and the donkey bumped into me and hid behind me. A man with an army came up to me.

The man nervously walked up to me and quietly said, 'Ogre, by the order of Lord Farquaad, I am authorised to place you both under arrest and transport you to a designed resettlement facility.'

The army behind the man made a run for it.

I said, 'You and what army?'

The man fled as fast as he could.

I turned away and the donkey followed me. He thanked me for all I had done. We got to know each other a little more, and all of a sudden he shouted, 'Can I stay with you? You're a mean, green fighting machine. Together we can scare the spit out of anybody who crosses us.'

I took a big breath and let out a big roar, right in front of the donkey. He did not seem scared at all. He said with great enthusiasm, 'Oh wow, that was really scary, and if you don't mind me saying, if that don't work, your breath will certainly get the job done - cos it stinks!'

Jessica Slack (11)
Hope Valley College, Hope Valley

A Day In The Life Of Donkey

A usual day of a hard-working donkey would start off by lugging the vegetables up the hill. But now, I'm free!

Shrek wakes me up at 8.30 (well it's later than I used to have to get up) and I eat some grass. After breakfast, we go and see if the princess is hungry, but she's already had three swamp toads, so we set off on our usual activity, taking Princes Fiona to her beloved Lord Farquaad.

Don't mention this to Shrek or anything, but how obvious does he want to make it that he has the hots for her? If he feels that way he should just tell her, cos quite frankly, he's makin' a right donkey of himself, and I should know!

Come dinner time everyone's starved, so Shrek rustles up some grub. Absolutely delicious it is spiderwebs served with rats' whiskers.

Honesty, Princess Fiona is a right little madam, belching and farting everywhere she goes.

We set off on the rest of the journey but not long after, we have to stop cos Fiona is scared of the dark. Hah, what a wuss! Wait, I'm scared of the dark, so we stop and make camp. I don't know what's goin' to happen next!

Rebecca Harby (12)
Hope Valley College, Hope Valley

A Day In The Life Of Shrek

The time I wake up varies, depending on whether I get a mob of people coming to attack me.

I always take a quick wallow in the swamp before breakfast. Living in the swamp is definitely the best place. I don't like people and you don't get many visitors here. The ones that do come, quickly leave.

Donkey usually comes round about 9 o'clock. He always has a new way to annoy me. Most days, Donkey brings Dragon round and we all go to a tournament.

At about 3 o'clock, we go t'shops. I never have to queue, so we're back at around 3.30 (again depending on whether anyone tries to kill me).

I usually get rid of Donkey, by letting rip, at about 7 o'clock. Then I can have a quiet tea, just the way I like it.

Ellie Hepworth (12)
Hope Valley College, Hope Valley

A Day In The Life Of Shrek

(An extract)

I wake at 8am to hear that stupid, annoying donkey singing one of his 'songs' again. Turning over, I try to cover my ears, so that I can't hear him. It isn't working, so I get up angrily, stomp over to the window and stand there watching Donkey wade through *my* swam to *my* house. 'Get out of my swamp now,' I say to him. He doesn't respond, but just keeps on ploughing through my swamp. Starting to quiver with irritation I roar, 'You stupid, insolent donkey, do you hear what I say? *Clear out of my swamp!*' I like my privacy, you see. I lead a simple, solitary life and I can't bear it when it is invaded by brainless idiots, like Donkey. After standing there for another few minutes watching him staring gormlessly into thin air, whilst swatting *my* flies with *his* tail, I decide to ignore him and start the day.

My typical day starts with a sludge shower, followed by breakfast. This usually consists of toast topped with slime and maggots, and to drink, lukewarm, dirty swamp water. After breakfast I have my morning pump. Ah, that's a good one, three fish - must be a personal best. After my morning pump, I decided to take a walk in the forest. Nine out of ten times I am unlucky and Donkey decides that he wants to come too. Today is one of those days.

I take one step out of the front door and surprise, surprise, there is Donkey bobbing up and down in front of me. Before I have time to say anything, he starts.

'Hey Shrek, where are you going?'

'Oh nowhere,' I say casually.

'Well, can I come with you?' says Donkey.

'*No,*' I say crossly.

'Oh pleeeeeeese,' brays Donkey. 'Come on, it'll be fun just you and me and ...'

I'm not in the mood for arguing with him so I sigh begrudgingly, 'OK, you can come, but *no* singing.'

I haven't been walking for long when I hear a very familiar voice singing a very familiar song. *'Donkey, can't you keep that dreaded mouth of yours closed?'* I bellow.

Donkey shrinks back in fear, but I don't say anything more to him as I am interested in something else. A small group of young fairy-tale creatures are walking slowly along the path. Quickly I hide behind a tree. Donkey follows. 'What are we doing here, Shrek?' he says.

'Just shut up,' I whisper in reply.

As the fairy-tale creatures pass the tree which I am hiding behind, I suddenly jump out and roar at the top of my voice, *'Grrrrrrrrr!'* The fairy-tale creatures run off in shock and I just stand there howling with laughter. Being an ogre, I absolutely despise fairy-tale creatures and there's nothing better than being able to give them a good scare. After I have got over my hysterics, my rumbling tummy reminds me of the time. It's 1pm. 'Lunchtime already!' I gasp. 'I'd better be going home.'

'Hey, what do I get for lunch when we get home?' inquires Donkey cheekily.

I shrug and say, 'Well you're not sharing my lunch, so you will have to find your own.'

Donkey whines and protests but I shut the door and go to get my lunch. After sitting outside my front door sulking for a while longer, Donkey eventually realises that I won't give in, so he goes to find his own lunch. My lunch today is a large plate of over-ripe fruit and vegetables accompanied by one of the fish asphyxiated by my morning pump, with yet another glass of swamp water - chilled is best for lunch. After my lunch I decide to take the rest of the afternoon easy, so I go for a mud bath in my swamp.

Sophie Carter (12)
Hope Valley College, Hope Valley

My Day As An England Footballer

Every day I wake up to find a tray of bacon and eggs in front of me, then my butler comes in and opens my curtains for me and pours me a glass of orange juice. I pick up my flip-up phone and look at the time, and realise I've got four hours until the match, England V Italy. *Not bad,* I think to myself. 'I'm pretty sure we'll win,' I say to my butler who, of course, was about to exit the room.

I get up, shake myself off, walk to my wardrobe and stare at my pride and joy ... my football kit. I get dressed in my posh clothes and go down the marble staircase, under the chandelier. Finally I get downstairs and I walk through the gigantic doors, out to the bottom of the massive garden to my pride and joy ... my Porsche. Well, my other pride and joy - I have so many now that I'm a footballer and can afford them.

I go out to town to buy clothes, jewellery and new footy boots, then I look at the time and rush home to collect my kit, and then I race off to the stadium. The match is due to start in exactly three-quarters of an hour, so I get changed and we go to the group meeting. I'm playing centre midfield.

We jog out onto the pitch and it's kick-off, and finally in the last minute, after everyone thinks it is going to be a draw, I run up with the ball, take a shot and the commentator screams out loud, 'And there's just a superb goal by England's centre midfielder. England have won the match by 1-0.'

That's worth a drink, I think - a glass of sparkling bubbly.

Jake Hickinson (11)
Hope Valley College, Hope Valley

A Day In The Life Of Homer

I live at 742 Evergreen Terrace. I normally wake up around 7am, if stupid Bart does not change my alarm. I start my day with bacon, coffee, sausage and egg, oh and mmm, donuts. Ahhh.

I then go and work at the nuclear power plant. I don't work, I just sleep and eat. After work I go to Moe's and have a few Duff beers, then I go home and have dinner and watch TV. I go to bed around 11pm and snuggle with Marge. I wake up in the night to get something to eat.

On Saturday, I sleep for most of the day and drink beer on the hammock, but stupid Flanders keeps waking me up.

In my family I have a wife, Marge; a boy, Bart; and two girls, Lisa and Maggie.

Jordan Lilley (12)
Hope Valley College, Hope Valley

A Day In The Life Of Pat Volumn

Every day has its own routine; it has to have because of who I am. With me being the captain of Arton United, I have to follow routine to keep me in tiptop condition. Every day I rise at 7am and breakfast on porridge, Weetabix, egg and bananas, this keeps me going until break time. I am 25 years old and was born on the Ivory Coast where it is warm every single day; these cold English days are terrible!

I am single and live in what is called a mansion in Essex. I have lived here for 5 years since I was signed for Arton United, the manager saw me playing on the beach and thought I would fit into his team well, so here I am. My mum and sister live here and fuss over me and spend my money. Dad and my brother are still back home enjoying the sunshine. One day I hope to retire and go back home to the sun and maybe set up a football academy there.

After breakfast I dress in plenty of layers and go to the training ground and see the team and manager, Albert Walker. We all work very hard and have pasta for lunch and then relax, play a few computer games and then perhaps go shopping.

I have a Labrador which I have to take on long walks in the evening and then end the day with a meal with my mum, sister and friends.

I go to sleep at 11pm and dream of feeling the sand under my feet as I play footy on the beach.

Tomorrow's routine will be a bit different because we are going to play in the AF Cup Final at the Trillenium Stadium. I shall get nervous because we are against our arch rivals Manchelsy United.

I am very superstitious, back home we would visit the village witch doctor, here I visit a fortune teller. Last week she told me that I would be lifting a silver cup after a long hard game. I wonder if this will come true?

Jonathan Swain (12)
Hope Valley College, Hope Valley

A Day In The Life Of Mr Johnson

Hello, let me introduce myself, my name is Mr Johnson, I live in the country a couple of miles from Buxton. I have been in jail once and the loony asylum twice. I live alone, I was married once but my wife, erm, mysteriously disappeared.

In my average day I usually get up about 9ish to the sound of my alarm clock, make breakfast, usually cornflakes and I watch my favourite breakfast time TV show, 'The Most Gory Car Accidents'.

I work part-time at the Extra sugar, chemicals, ice cream and chocolate factory and I love it!

I have to travel 4 to 5 miles to work and arrive about 11am. My job is to package the chocolate. I admittedly steal a few, spit in some, stick chewing gum and toenail clippings in them, but that's what anyone would do ... isn't it?

After an hour we have a lunch hour with free, yes *free* chocolate! I sometimes watch my colleagues eat hidden spit and stuff and it's hilarious watching them squirm and puke! Ha, ha, ha. I go home at 2 o'clock and go on the PlayStation for an hour (my favourite game is randomly killing helpless animals!)

Sometimes I do it for real, go down the park and chuck rocks at squirrels 'n' stuff. After a while the police normally get called and I get cautioned. I go home and watch TV while eating tea, usually watch, the most gory suicides.

If I get bored I usually do a prank call, something like calling the police and saying there is a psycho murderer in my house. I only get fined £50.

Usually I have a bath or shower around 8pm then watch horror movies for a few hours and, if it's a long film, I sometimes fall asleep on the sofa. I usually dream about little cute fluffy animals ... about to be run over by a lorry!

Robert Barnatt (12)
Hope Valley College, Hope Valley

A Day In The Life Of Avril Lavigne

The 21-year-old skater-girl reveals all. Avril's life - anything but ordinary, and that's putting it lightly. We catch up with Avril to see what goes on behind the scenes ...

Well, I'm all over the place flying here and there, going through different stuff every day, so this is just a fairly common example.

I usually wake up around 9.15 on a non-working day and grab a glass of orange juice. I then go downstairs; switch on my CD player - a Black Sabbath is usually in but at the moment it is 'No Thanks: The 70s Punk Rebellion Compilation'. I then chuck myself onto the couch and read the mail. Once that's been done I turn on MTV. I have a shower around 10.30 and have breakfast. I normally go for a can of beer and a PB & J sandwich. I bet by this time you're thinking, I'm one of those punk-druggie kind of people, but that's not me. I just like to be myself.

By this time my boyfriend, Deryck, has come down, we then have a good gossip at the kitchen table, whilst throwing down some cheese puffs. We hang out, do normal stuff, then I go to my study room and answer my fan mail. When I used to send fan mail to my idols, I used to be well upset because they didn't send anything back, that's probably when I do it.

At lunch, Deryck goes out to the recording studio. I then practise my guitar and sing and try out new songs in the basement. I've had it done up and it rocks. It's got great sound and projects real easy. I've got a writing block at the moment - no news means not much to write. I've got a tune but just no lyrics.

I often pop out after a bit of that, sometimes into the studio, but I normally go to Green Day, or Good Charlotte. I get on really well with Billie-Joe from Green Day. I help them out and they help me out. That's the way we work together, with Good Charlotte, I came up with one of the names of their songs off their first record.

If I go to the studio, I normally meet Simple Plan, my special guests from my tour.

When I'm on tour I stay in my bus almost all the time I'm not performing, hotels suck. With my bus, I've got everything with me and I never have to unpack.

Anyway, after going out I go back to my New York penthouse. I have a light snack, going for a choccy box for my snack and a can of beer - again. Honest, I'm not a junky.

I stay at home and sometimes lay on my king-sized bed, listening to my own music, over and over again, trying to find an idea for lyrics, or something.

Then Deryck arrives home in his new Koenigsegg, disturbing my peace. We usually go out in the evenings, we have exclusive VIP passes, that means we can get in wherever we want, whenever we want.

When I go out without Deryck, you'll find me partying with my mates, they say that I eat so bad they're almost too embarrassed to eat with me - apart from the fact I'm famous! I just chuck my fave grub down the hatch. That's my day done!

Katie Hodges (12)
Hope Valley College, Hope Valley

A Day In The Life Of ...

I wake early on weekdays, but have a lie-in on weekends. Max often wakes me up! I have a breakfast of rotten eggs on stale toast. Then I pop my head out of the window above the rubbish dump and breathe in the smelly, rotten air! It really wakes me up and I believe it's good for my skin.

I live with my dog, Max, who is very useful when I'm in a bad mood! He does most of the chores in my cave. He gets mardy, but I keep telling him that it's good for his health. I don't think he believes me though.

I regularly trash my house. I prefer a more 'not bothered' look for my dwelling!

At noon, Max and I go through the dump tunnel. It's Max's highlight of the day! We come out down in Whoville. I want revenge on all the Whos, so I go and cause as much trouble as possible: mixing up letters, tripping up Whos, that kind of thing. I find it very amusing!

When we get back up to Mount Crumpet, we check for waste and rubbish, if there is any, then we carry it up to the cave and load it into my home-made catapult. The waste is hurled at the ugly picture of Mayor Who.

After I've thoroughly amused myself, I get out my Whollow Pages and prank call all the Whos I hate. Then I think up evil schemes to ruin Christmas forever! I have tried and failed many times! After that, I sit in a dark corner and talk to myself about things that are troubling me.

To cheer myself up, I grab a cat and start strangling it in front of a loud speaker to wake up all the Whos! Then the majority of nights, I go to bed feeling highly satisfied!

Bryony Pullman (12)
Hope Valley College, Hope Valley

A Day In The Life Of Gary The Goldfish

Hi! I'm a goldfish! You may not think that that's very exciting so to prove you wrong I'll show you a day in the life of me.

I get up and swim round my home. There's a castle that I don't remember being there before. Maybe I'll look inside later. I wonder if Gertie would come?

Gertie's my friend. She always follows me and she looks exactly like me. She lives somewhere similar too but I can never join her because I always bang my head on an invisible wall.

What was I doing? Oh yes, I was looking at that diver over there. He doesn't seem to be doing much - just swimming to a chest but bubbles always knock him back before he gets there. He's not disheartened though. He just tries again (and again, and again). I wouldn't.

Hey! There's a castle! I don't remember that being there before. I'll go and check it out!

I've looked inside but it's all cramped and dark. Now it's feeding time! This is when flakes of food just fall from the sky, like a gift from a superior life form! I don't know how it happens, but suddenly it stops.

Now it's the next morning. I'm bored. You know, I could write a day in my life. People might be really interested, let's begin!

Hi, I'm a goldfish! You may not think that that's very exciting so to prove you wrong then here is a day in the life of me …

Jenny Benham (13)
King Edward VI School, Lichfield

When Does A Hobby Become An Obsession?

Joshua lived and died for caves.

By 8 years of age he had already bungee-jumped off a bridge and climbed up a mountain but by the time he was 17 Joshua was into caves. Really, seriously, deeply into caves. He loved their complex tunnels and underground streams. He loved their cool darkness and the refreshing silence broken only by the dripping of water from the cave roof. He marvelled at their size and had often hidden from trouble inside them. At school, all he thought about was caves and would only listen properly to the teacher if the subject of the lesson were anything to do with caves. Caves were his life.

Joshua had been planning his trip for months. His parents were both away and it was the perfect opportunity to put his plans into action. There was a cave just down the road from his house. He suspected that it was one of the biggest he had ever explored.

As he stood in front of it, the sheer size made him shudder with anticipation. Attaching the rope to his waist he started to descend ... down, down, down, it was getting much darker and much colder ... down, down, down, he would reach the bottom soon, he was sure of it. Then, suddenly, he felt something slacken. He looked up and saw ... a slate, razor-sharp, cutting into the rope.

'Noooooooooooooooo!' Joshua screamed as he fell. Black! It was over.

Joshua lived and died for caves. Really!

Robbie Beck (13)
King Edward VI School, Lichfield

A Day In The Life Of Me!

A day in the life ... ? I don't know. I'm not going to write a made up story, I'm going to tell you the genuine tale of a day in the life of ... me!

It's Saturday. I get up at 9am and have breakfast, then I get dressed. I bet you're asleep already! Truthfully, my life is *very* uninteresting! Well nobody ever said I had to tell the truth I suppose:

It is Saturday morning; I wake up bright and early; the sun is already streaming in through my curtains. Something feels different this morning, somehow special and exciting. I leap out of bed although it's only 6.30 and fling open the curtains.

Sunlight pours into the room! Birds are singing in the trees around the house. No one is about. One of the birds comes and perches on the window sill. It's very brightly coloured - blue, yellow and green. I stare into its eyes for a moment or two - mesmerised. Suddenly I feel a tingling. It starts at my toes and slowly works all the way up to my head. Even the very ends of my hair seem to be tingling. I stretch out and push the window wide open. I find myself stepping out onto the ledge. I look down, I don't know what I'm doing but somehow I don't feel a bit scared. Then I stretch out my arms and topple off the sill.

There is a moment of terror as I feel myself tumbling but then I am floating up, up and away; high above the trees and houses, arms outstretched and I suddenly realise that I'm flying! It feels amazing like nothing anybody's ever experienced before!

Well there is a day in the life of me. Just not exactly an ordinary one!

Liz Hollis (13)
King Edward VI School, Lichfield

A Day In The Life Of ...

9.30 - We set off for school. One of my arms comes off so I must wait till Victoria Pritt Sticks it back on.

10.00 - We reach school and I play with my fellow Barbie sisters. Hula Barbie, Ballerina Barbie and Ken. I don't know why everyone thinks I like him so much. Past the perfect hair and constant smile is an arrogant, self-centred ... you know.

12.00 - It's lunch and yet again I have an assortment of ketchup and pizza stuck in my hair.

2.00 - Victoria's mum comes to pick her and her vile playmate up. Susan, the face of all evil. At the grand old age of four enjoys mountain biking, rock music and already wants a tattoo on her left arm.

2.11 - Now we must 'play'.

Must ... keep ... smiling ... I think to myself, as my head is plucked off. Great! Now I have no arm and no head.

I try to close my eyes.

The flush.

I think Susan forgot to flush on purpose. I come out looking browner than before.

3.00 - Next in my schedule is my hairdressing session, with budding hairdresser Victoria. With a flash of her safety scissors and a quick whizz over with the felt tip, there we have it, a whole new stubbly hair do, with pink and green highlights. Next she does my make-up with her mum's lipstick. I end up looking like there's been an explosion in a tomato factory.

As my last word I'll tell you one phrase that will change your life forever. 'Being plastic, it's not fantastic'.

Pippa Revell (13)
King Edward VI School, Lichfield

Ghost Girl

I sat at the back on my own. My head hung low and my mousy brown hair hung over my face, shielding me from the world. Everyone around me was talking and laughing with their friends - populars, goths, geeks, boffins ...

And then there was me. Sarah Peters. An invisible plain Jane with no voice, no personality, no nothing. I was alone, no friends, no family, no one who cared. People didn't even see me let alone like me. I was unknown to nearly everyone.

I pulled the scruffy purple book from my bag. My precious scrapbook. It wasn't my diary; it was the beautiful, intelligent Scarlet Jones'. Every time I found a picture of someone on the ground or in a magazine I would put it in my scrapbook and I'd pretend the people were my friends. In real life I was Sarah, but in my book I was the amazing Scarlet ...

'What's this Ghostie?' said a voice behind me. A hand snatched my book away. I turned to see it in the grubby hands of Stacey. She was the biggest bully in Knightly and took a special interest in me. I had thought about telling someone about her, but who wanted to listen? I was just boring, invisible Sarah. I could feel my heart pounding in my ears and face burning as Stacey and her friends roared in laughter at the contents of my book.

'Look, she has imaginary friends!' they snorted.

A flash of confidence suddenly buzzed in my head. I wasn't just Sarah. I was the amazing Scarlet, who could stand up to anyone.

'Give that back right now, you stupid cow!' I screamed.

Stacey and her gang froze and stared at me in disbelief. She slowly strode up to me and I began to shake with fear as she towered over me.

'I'm sorry, Stacey. I didn't mean it. I'm sorry!' I cowered as they pushed me into the forbidden area of the field.

My words were met with a showering of punches and I fell to the floor instantly. I tried to stop them but was too weak to do anything. They kicked me continuously, as if I were a football. I didn't stand a chance ...

It was days later when a teacher finally found me, surrounded in a pool of blood. I was taken to hospital but it was too late. I was dead but nobody cared. So it's just me, alone again. Ghost girl.

Holly Youlden (13)
King Edward VI School, Lichfield

Tottio God Of Landscape

Tottio married Plantasia on top of Beauty Mountain, but Tottio's brother Plutonion was jealous and to spite Tottio Plutonion killed Plantasia. Tottio was distraught and declared war with Plutonion, which according to Ancient Greek law, had to be settled in combat with the loser forfeiting his life.

Plutonion assembled an army of giants but Tottio knew Plutonium's tricks and gathered an army of hydras, each with five vicious heads.

On the morning of the battle the two armies smashed into one another but the hydras were strong. Soon the giants fell dead in huge mounds and a great river of blood ran through the battlefield. Tottio was the victor so Plutonium's life was forfeit, but as Tottio lifted his sword he realised that he could not go through with it and he walked away from the battlefield.

Tottio remained unhappy because his beloved Plantasia was still dead. After many years he returned to the battlefield and saw that the giants' bodies had turned to stone and grassed over forming the hills and mountains we see today. The river of blood now ran clear and the mouths and organs of every giant formed cave systems and potholes.

Drawn back to Beauty Mountain, where he had married Plantasia, Tottio prayed for his beloved Plantasia to return, but he heard a voice saying, 'Plantasia can never again become mortal but because of compassion shown to your brother, you will live forever as the landscape and your wife will be immortal as the plants, and you will both join the gods in the heavens.'

Sam Atkins (13)
King Edward VI School, Lichfield

Myth - Why There Are Tides At Sea

There were once two brothers who were constantly fighting and arguing. They argued so much that they had even forgotten what they were arguing about. They argued everywhere; at home, on the street, in towns, cities, anywhere.

One day they were at the holy temple in Ihop, where they lived. Halfway through the service they suddenly started arguing. They fought, swore, broke statues of the gods and threw holy books at each other.

This greatly angered the gods, especially Insfos the god of the Earth who was very vain and did not like having his statues broken. One day while the brothers were arguing Insfos came down from Heaven to Earth before them.

As a punishment for their crimes, Insfos decided to kill them. He cast one brother into the water to drown and the other was buried in the ground to suffocate. However, Sofsni, Insfos' evil brother decided to ruin Insfos' plans and made the fighting brothers immortal. They therefore survived for many thousands of years, unable to escape and one day became a part of the sea and the land, and controlled them as gods of the sea and land, with the help of Sofsni.

However this great punishment did not stop them from arguing and so every day Sea tries to drown his brother Land by covering him with water and Land tries to dry Sea out by covering him with soil and sand. That is why there are tides at sea.

Robin Nowell (13)
King Edward VI School, Lichfield

Butterfly

In Ancient Greek times, there was a great god. Her name was Butterfly. She was a beautiful and powerful god of wind. She sent tornadoes and hurricanes across the globe.

As she was young, she was stupid. She misused her powers and for that the gods decided to strip her of her powers but the winds warned her of this and so she flew away and hid herself in the forest.

A great male god went to find her; he trudged through the enchanted forest until he finally found her. Nobody had warned him of her secret weapon, her beauty. The minute he saw her, he was under her spell. Her beauty paralysed him, when she saw him though, she fell in love. She unwove her spell and set him free.

They both lived happily in the forest together for years. He used his powers to make sure that the forest had enough to drink by making rain cloud to bring a light shower. She used hers to blow away the clouds when the forest had had enough so the sun could shine down. They secretly became married and she fell pregnant. The other gods had not forgotten about her and sent a group of female gods to stop her. They chopped her up and scattered her body parts around the globe. Each part burst into butterflies.

Her husband never got over her, the rain is his tears. When every butterfly beats its wings at the same time it creates a hurricane or tornado, this is part of her revenge.

Mat Wannell (13)
King Edward VI School, Lichfield

The Extraordinary Box

My myth is all about a magical box that is owned by someone that no one knows. When the level of evilness gets to a high volume, all over the world, then the box is opened. The box sucks up all the sinful people and all evil in the world including objects. This disastrous experience happens exactly once every two months. It causes the *hurricane*. The box isn't always very precise. This then makes the world disturbed as it sucks up some good things like houses, animals and some of the good, helpful, cheerful people. This disturbs the world because nobody knows what they have done wrong or where they have gone. The owner of the box has never been found and never will be.

Every time there is a hurricane the box grows bigger and bigger, and when the bearer gets older and older, the box gets (grows) better, with more jewels on it. If the bearer of the box is ever found then all evil concealed will be set free.

If all evil is released the world will become an awful, disgusting and scary place to live. If too many people are evil and the box gets too big, the box and bearer will take over the world forever.

The moral to my myth is that it's best to be good. If you're evil you will ruin your life and get sucked up forever. Hurricanes aren't devastating as they are protecting the world from evil even though innocent lives may be lost.

Harriet Thompson (13)
King Edward VI School, Lichfield

My Myth

Once upon a time in a small village years and years ago, lived a god named Thesaurus. He lived in the times of the depression where everything was black and white and the world was boring. Thesaurus was an excellent painter and sculptor and used to create amazing drawings with his black and white paint.

One day Thesaurus came up with an amazing idea, colour! If he could make things different colours the world would be exciting but he didn't know how to make the colour. Thesaurus had a friend named Blue who was a science genius, he gave Thesaurus the idea of a spectrum and when the sun would hit the paint, a beautiful set of colours would all appear.

When Thesaurus came home he tried this out and it worked and he produced pots and pots of coloured paints. He was so grateful he ran to Blue's house and said, 'I will name one of my most famous colours after you!' Thesaurus got out his paint brushes and started painting his house, people came all over the world to admire this wonderful phenomenon.

One day Thesaurus was visited by a great god, the greatest Megolly and she spoke on how amazing it was and she gave Thesaurus a mission, he had to paint the sky.

Thesaurus was excited by this challenge but scared. He knew that if he did it wrong he would be punished. He mixed in all his nicest colours and made a beautiful colour and named it after his friend 'Blue'. Thesaurus got started and painted the whole sky and that's why the sky is blue.

Megan Cross (13)
King Edward VI School, Lichfield

Rhano And The Tsunami

One day Rhano, a huge, young, very strong god with a brown, short beard and a curled moustache, was sitting in his most comfortable cloud, watching the wonderful Earth spin around. He was just thinking what his next mission would be. His duty was to protect all living beings. A gigantic flaming meteor came soaring past him and headed for the big blue ocean.

Rhano knew exactly what would happen and knew his task would be difficult. A massive tsunami of waves travelling at extreme speeds would occur and would kill an immense amount of living life. He proudly got out off his cloud and using his super speed of light speed, he swiftly headed for the mountains. He got there and used his amazing strength, he heaved a colossal mountain out of the ground and headed swiftly back to the ocean, only this time he could not travel as fast with the mountain in his arms. It took him a few minutes this time and the waves were closing in fast on land. He did not have long. He finally reached the coast, the waves crashing in; about to hit land and Rhano threw the mountain at a certain angle in front of the waves. This made them speed in the opposite direction. This part of the land was saved; he now had to deal with the waves that had sped the other way from the meteor.

He used his speed of light power to travel across the ocean and then to the nearest mountains. He heaved one out of the ground and struggled it back to the coast where the waves would crash and he waited for them to come.

When they came he could throw the mountain at them to send them in the opposite direction. When they came he did this and went back to his cloud to watch the two waves crash into each other in the middle of the ocean.

Stuart Clayton (13)
King Edward VI School, Lichfield

Jane's Diary Beats The Bully

'Oi Fatty,' shouted Will.

'Stop calling me that,' replied Jane.

'No, why should I?' yelled Will.

Even though the days were beautiful and bright, Jane's days were dull and grey. Jane hated school now she was being bullied. She knew she was overweight and that's why she was being bullied. Jane didn't tell anyone she was being bullied, even her best friend Sarah had started to pick on her. Jane always kept a diary, that was until her mother found it ...

13th May 2005

Dear Diary,

I was in tears again at school because of Will and Sarah. They started to call me 'Fatty' again. Sometimes I even think about killing myself. I should really tell Mum but it's too hard.

Write to you soon, Jane.

At teatime, Jane's mother could see she was upset and asked Jane what was wrong.

Jane just said, 'Nothing, it's hay fever.' When Jane had finished eating, she went upstairs and cried herself to sleep.

The next day Jane realised her diary was missing!

Her mum had read it and found out about her being bullied. Jane burst into tears and her mother comforted her. Jane's mum talked to her about being bullied and they both decided to go to the school the next day.

The head teacher, Mr Brown, told Jane and her mum he already knew about the bullying and he had tried to stop it before, but it just started again. Mr Brown said he would talk to Sarah and Will about it, which he did.

Jane and her mum decided to lose some weight together and over the next few months, Jane lost over 2 stone. Jane wasn't bullied again, as they realised how nice she was and Sarah was her friend again.

Laura Wheeler (12)
Kingsbury School, Tamworth

Where Are We Going?

Barry and Bill are best friends, they had been since playgroup, and every year their two families went on holiday abroad. This year they were going to a rainforest in Australia.

They reached Birmingham airport at 5 o'clock in the morning. They checked in, looked on the board to see when their flight was and saw it had been delayed by an hour. Barry and Bill got stuck looking after Bill's little sister, Holly.

On the plane Bill felt sick. 16 hours later they landed in Australia at Sydney airport.

The two families went to collect their luggage. They had hired a car so they could drive to different places.

The first place was a little cottage outside of the rainforest. For the rest of the day they played outside of the cottage to explore.

Barry and Bill went for a walk in the rainforest. They didn't know what time it was so they carried on walking. They were getting tired so they tried to find their way back to the cottage.

Late at night, Barry and Bill were still trying to get back to the cottage. Back at the cottage their parents were getting worried.

The next morning, Barry and Bill were still lost. Their parents called the police and 30 minutes later the police came. Their parents were still tense about whether their children would be safe.

About 10 minutes later the police found them lying asleep against a tree. They walked out of the forest safe and went home.

Robert Ovens (12)
Kingsbury School, Tamworth

My Diary

Welcome to my diary, these are the best 4 days of the year.

The first day

The hottest day of the year. All day I lay there in the sun. All I could hear was the aeroplanes going over in the blue sky with no clouds in sight. Then the sweet smell of next-door's barbecue, the sizzling sausages. Mmm, they were making me hungry.

The second day

Next I was walking down the road on a windy autumn day. I could hear the wind whistling around my ears, at the same time blowing the leaves down the road. As I was crossing the road, brightly coloured washing caught the corner of my eye. The horse chestnut tree was swishing from side to side with the conkers hitting the ground and rolling away.

The third day

That bitter cold winter night way back in December. I was walking down the road with my big coat on. As I walked down I could hear the snow crunching at my feet. Pitter-patter, the rain washing the snow down the road, into the drain.

The best ever

It was the arrival of my new horse. It was the best looking mare I had ever seen. She was as white as snow with brown spots on her with a pretty head. On her head was a black star. Her mane was white and flowed in the wind.

That was it, the rest was school and the normal.

Sarah Snazle (12)
Kingsbury School, Tamworth

Me!

30th June

It's a roasting hot day so why am I sat under an oak tree being protected by the sun's glossy leaves? Well I burn easily and look like a tomato and I'm writing. A proper story. The problem is I don't know what to write.

31st June

Here I am again under the oak. I know, I'll write about *me* but who would want to read about a boring girl whose life has nothing interesting happen? I could make up a fairy tale about me.

20th August

I've written it. I save the fairies from the greedy goblins. I'm a one-girl wonder. It's being published soon. I'll read some ... I was surrounded by daisies and rich green grass. It was like a fairy tale world it was. Fairies in their pretty dresses fluttering about. It was paradise.

25th August

They love it. Shops have sold out. I've made lots of money. I'm famous. I've got a meeting about it later. I wonder what it's about.

2nd September

They want to make it into a film. I said I'd love it to. The problem is they want me to star in it! Me! I'm not even an actress. Oh no!

3rd September

I'm going to star in the movie. I'll be even more famous. I've got too many lines to learn. I don't know how I am going to do it.

25th September

I've started to film the movie. It's an amazing experience. I won't need a diary anymore. I've got a whole life full of interviews and being famous. To think this started under an oak tree. Hey, it's a story in a story!

Jessica Nash (12)
Kingsbury School, Tamworth

A Hard Life

As I walk slowly down the street, leaves crunch underfoot. The snow falls softly onto my nose and trickles down my cheek. It drips down and soaks my bare foot. My ripped, battered clothes blow in the wind.

I walk down the street looking in all the windows. I see a family sitting around a fire next to a twinkling tree. The roasting marshmallows drip off the stick and into the fire. It makes a cloud of smoke which drifts up the chimney and disappears into the sky.

I carry on walking. The house looks dark and gloomy. As I look in a new emotion takes over. I feel sad and happy at the same time. I think about my old family and the night when I lost them. My life was destroyed. I'm all I've got left now and that's not much.

I think about Tom and Maggie, my dear Maggie. Why is life so hard? What have I done to deserve this? Does anyone know I used to have a life? Now I'm just the tramp.

My legs are getting tired, I need to lie down. Thoughts keep flooding through my head. I lie down on a bench, my eyelids are heavy. I drift slowly into a deep sleep. I sit up and everything around me is light. I feel a pat on my shoulder, I turn around and there is Maggie with Tom hand in hand. I pinch myself but I'm not dreaming …

Holly Cant (12)
Kingsbury School, Tamworth

The Fall

A thin and quite scrawny boy of 14 perched comfortably in the peak of a grand oak tree watching the horrendous weather. Kyle enjoyed the sound of the raindrops on the leaves of the tree and best of all not being at home.

Kyle had dark ginger hair which was always scruffy because he never had time to comb or gel his hair. He had a long, crooked nose, thin lips and hazel eyes.

Kyle reckoned life couldn't get much worse. His parents were arguing and he thought it was because of him.

Kyle took a deep breath and exhaled the invigorating air as lightning crackled through the sky. He began to climb down. Suddenly a branch he was hanging on broke from his grasp. It was a long fall. He hit the ground headfirst; there was an enormous crack and excruciating pain.

Three weeks later he awoke to the dim surroundings of a hospital room. There was a strong aroma of disinfectant among the air. He couldn't move, he heard his mother crying outside the room and his dad speaking.

'It's okay dear,' he reassured his wife.

Well, thought Kyle, *at least my parents are together still, that's got to be one advantage.*

Everything he had been sad about seemed so small now. He supposed he could be seriously hurt, but it could be worse. A crazy theory came across his mind, he could be dead. His parents stared at him through the window with solemn faces, it could be true ...

Reuben Butler (12)
Kingsbury School, Tamworth

The Tailor

I was driving my Aston Martin when I heard my police radio squawking.
'Control to 1658, do you copy?'
I replied, '1658 to control, carry on.'
'We have just received a call to say the mass murderer, John Stone, has escaped prison. We are worried because you were the one that put him inside and we think that he's after you. Please return to headquarters immediately for briefing.'
I put my foot down and the engine was roaring like a charging bull. My speedometer was coming up to 120mph. My driving skills were still as good as ever.
I parked in the underground car park and walked into the headquarters through the back entrance. I entered Jackie's office. Suddenly the buzzer sounded. That meant to go and see M for a briefing.
I sat down on the large leather chair.
'What are you having?' M asked.
'I'll have a whiskey please.'
M said, 'You'll meet an informant in Cuba's harbour in three days' time. He will tell you everything you need to know about John Stone. I am giving you these handguns and a passport.'
I slowly started to walk out of the room when she threw me some keys.
I asked, 'What are these for?'
She replied, 'Your new plane. Go to Q and get it.'

I was looking for the best hotel in Cuba and I found the Gorinzaz. This looked appealing. I booked the penthouse suite. I had just unpacked and felt hungry so I called for some food and a tailor so I could have a suit made to measure. A knock came at the door, it was the tailor. It was John Stone. He didn't know who I was but I knew who he was. As soon as he came in I pulled out my Glock and shot him twice in-between the eyes.

Joe Coupe (12)
Kingsbury School, Tamworth

Shark Attack

On a very hot sunny day two men decided to go on a boat trip around Oceania. They had a list off a friend of all the equipment they would need to go deep-sea diving. Their friend had told them that there was a shop nearby that sold all the things on the list so they decided to go and check it out. The shop was full of things to buy and they'd soon found all the things they wanted.

They boarded the ship to Oceania. When they got there one of the men got his diving gear on and dived in. He saw the immediate beauty of the blue clear sea as he swam about looking at the different species of fish. Nobody could see in the distance. There was a great white shark and it knew that the diver was in the distance. The diver was so amazed at what he was witnessing, he did not realise that he had cut his hand and blood was coming from the wound. The shark caught the scent of the blood with its big, sensitive nostrils and charged towards him. The diver looked up to see the last sight he would ever see - the shark's opened jaws. It sunk its razor-sharp teeth into his leg and his back and wouldn't let go. The blue beautiful sea that surrounded the boat turned into a bloodbath.

Fortunately the shark backed away from the body, carrying a chunk of flesh in its mouth. As they pulled him out of the water, they checked for a pulse, there was a slight beat. They rushed him to hospital as quickly as possible. This man survived with major scars to his leg and back. He claimed it wasn't the shark's fault and proceeded with research on sharks and he loved them despite what one of the creatures had done to him.

Ben Evans (11)
Kingsbury School, Tamworth

The List

It was the end of summer; I was lying under an oak tree watching a leaf float down towards earth. It made me think of the past summer. What I had done. I remembered my list, my summer list. It had everything I wanted to do this summer.

I ran home as fast as I could; it was a struggle, but I finally reached the door. As I opened it, I could smell a waft of Sunday lunch. Lamb, potatoes and of course, the gravy. You could almost feel it dripping down your throat. I ran upstairs, straight into my room and opened my paper draw to find my summer list. It wasn't there!

I opened the window 'cause all this running had made making me hot. I heard the door bang shut. I jumped round and there it was, my list on the back of the door. Then I remembered I'd put it there for safekeeping. I looked at it; it had all the things on and they were: learn to fly, run a marathon and visit another planet.

I lay back on my bed and wondered why I had ticked them all, I thought back. I did learn to fly: I flew the cardboard box plane me and my brother Jimmy had made. I was the pilot and he was the commander. I'd also ran a marathon. Jimmy had taken one of my marbles and I'd chased him round all day. I also went to Zog. I turned the plane into a rocket. I had done everything; my mind was at rest.

Then I heard, 'Johnny, dinner!' and I ran downstairs.

Steven Carter (12)
Kingsbury School, Tamworth

My School Trip Disaster

One summer morning I was sitting, trying to keep myself awake. I was waiting to go on a school trip, without my best friend. She had said she couldn't come because she was ill.

'Flight 2 can come now.'

'It's time to go,' I whispered to myself.

'Hi.'

I thought I heard my best friend behind me. I turned round and to my surprise, there stood Sam. A big smile crept across my face and I threw my arms around her. 'I thought you couldn't come,' I said, still smiling.

'You didn't fall for that, did you? Come on then, we are going to miss the plane,' shouted Sam, not laughing anymore.

'Get your passports out quick,' I said, rummaging through my bag.

'Right, run!' Sam yelled.

'Finally,' I whispered. I was out of breath; I don't think Sam could even talk.

'Can I have your passports please?' asked a strange-looking lady.

'Yeah, sure,' Sam replied.

'This is out of date,' said the lady.

'OK, can we do anything?' I said with embarrassment.

'No, sorry,' replied the lady.

We told our teacher we couldn't go because our passports were out of date, so she phoned our moms to pick us up.

I went with Sam the next day to get a new passport. Sam said she was sorry. I asked her what for, and she said it was her fault we missed the trip because her passport was out of date.

Danielle Purves (12)
Kingsbury School, Tamworth

Dear Diary

Dear Diary,

I woke up to find that it was another cold, miserable morning, so I put my blue thick sweater on and decided after a while to go for a long walk.

When I was walking, I could hear and see the colourful, crispy leaves crunching with every step I made. I could see in an open window, people and also children, by a warm, glowing fire, smiling. I had to suddenly stop. I had just noticed something!

I had just realised that a strange man, who was wearing black woolly clothes, was following me wherever I went. I started to run, super fast, but he was still there, coming straight towards me really quickly. It seemed to me that he was going as fast as a car.

By this time, I had become extremely tired and wanted to collapse, but I just couldn't. I finally did and fell to the rough, hard ground. After a few minutes I realised that the strange-looking man had vanished. *But how had he?* I thought to myself.

I decided to make my way back home. On my way home though, I noticed the man again. This time he had a sharp, silver-looking knife in his hand, so I really got worried and very nervous. I fell loudly to the ground again. But this time the ground was soft and really nice. I realised I was back home. *What a relief!* I thought to myself. *Was it a dream, or was it really real?*

I will think about it and tell you tomorrow.

See you, Diary,

        Lucy.

Lucy Foster (12)
Kingsbury School, Tamworth

The Monster

It was a dark, cold night. I was on my way home. It was freezing. That's when it happened. That's when I saw him, the man nicknamed 'The Monster'. I ran home as fast as I could, shaking.

The kids in the village say he only comes out at night. That's when he kills. That's why you never go into the woods. That's his lair. No one ever escapes.

I've recently moved into this village. After the stories I've heard, I want to move out. I am aged 12, have brown hair and my name's Jordan. That's about it. Except I cause a lot of trouble when I'm playing outside.

After looking nearly everywhere for my friends after lunch, I couldn't find them, so I went into the woods. Very bad mistake. As soon as I went in, I saw him. He chased me. I was really scared. I had never run so fast. I saw an opening in the trees. I wasn't going to make it; he was going to kill me. He was so close to me. He suddenly fell, he had tripped over!

I made it out of the woods and walked back to the village. I was shaking. I saw my friends. I told them what happened and they said the monster was them. They had got big boots from their home and were wearing a cloak. I didn't notice the hair, because my first instinct was to run. They did it for a joke. I was so annoyed.

I've never been their friend since. I will scare them next time. I will leave it to your imagination what I will do. I will get revenge!

Jordan Hinds (12)
Kingsbury School, Tamworth

Gemma And The Green Hairy Monster

It was a dark and windy evening. The thunder rumbled in the distance. Lightning shot down like the fork of the Devil. Rain hammered on the rooftops. It seemed as if the peace would never return.

This all happened in Botts End. This usually quiet village had an unusual occupant within the cosy houses in a row, the little shops in a bundle and the winding streets. He was a monster.

Gemma, a friendly child, always thought she had the calling to be a heroine; unfortunately that calling never rang out. But she didn't realise its imminence.

One sunny afternoon, everything was peaceful until the roar of the monster shattered the windows of the cosy cottages on Botts End. The monster stormed through the village, leaving a trail of destruction in his wake. He ruined the picturesque view with the dust that flew off the crushed houses. He left devastation and destruction.

The next day, the monster returned to finish the job. He was just about to crush a shop when Gemma heard her calling and ran over to him. She screamed, 'Oi, listen to me.'

The monster looked down at Gemma with a surprised expression.
'Why are you destroying our village?' asked Gemma calmly.
'Because I have a son and I was trying to protect him.'
'That's no reason for this.'
'I know, I'm sorry.'
'That's OK.'

The rest of the day was spent by all the occupants of Botts End rebuilding their future.

Keeley Humphries (12)
Kingsbury School, Tamworth

Accident

It was a scorching day, the smell of fresh-cut grass was going up my nose, making my eyes water because of hay fever.

We were getting ready to see a skewbald cob. All the others we had seen were too small. I had a funny feeling this pony was going to be the one.

He was lovely! He had the thickest tail you have ever seen. His name was Cleo and he was now mine! I fell in love with him as soon as I saw him and the previous owner said he had no vices.

'Monday, I will take him on a hack!' I announced.

We took Cleo home so he could settle.

Monday came, it was a lovely day. The forecast said it was going to be a fine day. I tacked him up and went on a long hack.

It started to become cloudy and drops of rain landed on us. The rain got heavier. Cleo started to misbehave, so I got off to lead him. Lightning struck and seconds later the thunder. Cleo shot forward, I fell funny and broke my leg. I had still got the reins, but I had to let go. I was on my own, hoping Cleo would find somewhere safe.

Fortunately Cleo galloped home, finding my mom. She eventually found me in pain. She rang an ambulance straight away.

Bad news soon came. They said I would never be able to ride gain. So Cleo and I went to lessons and learnt how to do carriage racing, and we became champions.

Charlotte Perry (12)
Kingsbury School, Tamworth

Unexpected Surprise

Dear Diary,

Am I too old for a diary? Oh well ... the boys are out, so it's just me and Charlotte here in the flat. That reminds me, we had a big disaster last week.

Mr Bennet, the flat owner, came on Monday to collect the rent. We weren't expecting him and rushed around looking for money. The rent was £1,200 for the four of us. We came up with £100.

His words were, 'If you don't come up with the money by Saturday, you're out!'

By Wednesday we'd tried everything. Rob came back from the pub and he had an idea. The pub was having a talent show and the prize was £1,500. It was on a Friday night. Rob and Bill were going to perform.

The show started at 8pm; we arrived there early. At the end of the room was a stage. The guys practised, we sat down and watched. A lot of people started coming. Everyone was ready to begin and Rob and Bill were on, they looked really nervous.

Everyone had soon finished. The presenter announced, 'You are officially the worst singers in town!' We had won! Rob and Bill were given the money. Everyone was laughing at them. Bill ran off the stage, Rob followed him. They were totally embarrassed. At least we had the money though. I don't know what we'll do next time we have to pay the rent; we'll have to wait and see.

Freisha Patel (12)
Kingsbury School, Tamworth

Spooky Woods

My mates and I were trying to conquer the world, but it all ended in a shambles …

It is Friday 26th June 2008. Dangerous creatures are lurking in the distance: tigers, wolves and cheetahs. They are all waiting to pounce. They are waiting for us. When they see us, they will charge and eat us, we're dead meat.

We had to act fast. We had to pack up the camp and get it into our bag. I had some breakfast. It was cold and wet and we needed to get to the haunted house, where we should be safe, well, hopefully.

We started to move. The house was six miles ahead. It was cold and wet and we really needed to stop, if we didn't, we would lose a group member. He was dying of hypothermia. So we stopped and put him in a sleeping bag and warmed him up.

We arrived safely at the house, now we needed to check out the house. It was old and was built in the 1960s, which was a long time ago. We were cold and wet. We wished we were back home, back where we started.

One of my mates said that he had seen a ghost and that it had tried to speak. We just ignored it. That's when we found out that it was haunted. We soon packed our belongings and went.

We headed for the Atlantic Ocean. We needed to go home. We missed our families and wanted to see our loved ones.

Rhys Yates (12)
Kingsbury School, Tamworth

My Monologue

I'm made of bricks, I have a shiny blue door and windows too. No prizes for guessing what I am, yep you've got it I'm just a dull brick house. But one not so dull thing happened to me once. Let me tell you about it.

Well, it all started off as an ordinary day. I was just standing around as houses do, not bothering anyone. But suddenly two strange little pigs came running along, I had no idea what was going on, they just ran straight inside me slamming my lovely blue door! I mean what had I ever done to them?

Anyway a little later along came this very scary wolf. He started shouting, 'If you don't let me in I'll huff and I'll puff and I'll blow your house down!'

This was one dumb wolf, everyone knows you can't blow bricks down. But he tried and obviously failed so he stormed away angrily.

Later he came back with a ladder. He propped it up against me and started to climb up onto my roof. I wondered what he was going to do, I was getting kind of nervous. But all he did was slide down my chimney. There was nothing he could do, only kill the little pigs! Instead of hearing the pigs scream I surprisingly heard the wolf scream!

The wolf never came out again but that's probably because the pigs ate him for their dinner!

Rebecca Jones (12)
Kirkby College, Nottingham

How The Tortoise Got Its Shell

Once there was a tortoise that was absolutely rubbish at hide-and-seek, but he played for the fun of it. One day the tortoise and his friends the rabbit, snake and bee were playing hide-and-seek and because he'd lost again his friends made fun of him, so he thought how he could camouflage himself so he could win and not be made fun of.

Suddenly he had an idea, so he grabbed a rock as big as his body and took it home. He grabbed his dad's chainsaw and made arm holes, leg holes, a tail hole and a head hole and he hollowed it out. Then he put it on and it was a perfect fit.

The next day he went to play hide-and-seek, his friends still made fun of him, but he went on to win and win and win. His friends started to get jealous and they decided to ignore him.

After a month the rabbit, snake and bee started to feel ashamed of themselves because they knew they were in the wrong, so they went and apologised and made friends again and they went on playing hide-and-seek and the tortoise sometimes made it easy to find him so they wouldn't fall out again.

Kallum Beazley (12)
Kirkby College, Nottingham

The Blue Skin

It all started on May 5th 2004. Jimmy and Robert were walking through the woods when they heard a strange rustle from a bush. They walked towards the bush and a skinny, blue arm shot out and squeezed round Jimmy's neck. Jimmy went blue in the face and screamed but Robert picked up a plank of wood and smacked the creature in the face. It jumped out of the bush and growled.

It had a bent back and leathery blue skin. Robert bravely took a photo and darted off. Jimmy followed but he wasn't very fast and fell down a hole. He was trapped down there for an hour. It grabbed Jimmy out of the hole and showed off his massive teeth, Jimmy closed his eyes.

'I can't do it,' it said.

Jimmy was shocked to hear it speak English. 'What can't you do?' asked Jimmy.

'I just can't kill you, even though you humans wiped out my species 200 years ago,' it replied. 'I'm the only blue skin left.'

Jimmy felt sorry for the creature and said he'd like to help it.

'My burrow was destroyed when you humans built on this land,' it explained.

Jimmy looked over to the building site which the creature was referring to and then Jimmy had an idea. He saw a pneumatic drill and told the creature his plan to drill a hole.

Robert came with the police and shouted for the monster to surrender. Jimmy protected it but a tank came towards them. A massive rumble cracked the earth open and a huge hole opened up, it fell down the hole. He waited and heard a very faint, 'Thank you human.'

Jay Roberts (13)
Kirkby College, Nottingham

The Porridge Am I

I remember it like it was yesterday, even though it was only this morning. Well, first thing I remember was being poured into this stupid little baby bowl and next to me was my mum and dad. We sat there waiting for our destiny, well basically being eaten. (In case you didn't know by now I'm porridge, plain, boring porridge.)

First to come down was a small overweight bear bouncing down the stairs. Yeah, like he needed any more porridge. He was followed by this huge, ginormous, as big as a house, bear. He picked up a spoon and took a big scoop out of my dad.

'This porridge is too hot,' he moaned. 'Let's go for a walk,' he continued.

Finally, they were gone, now all I needed to do was get out of this darn bowl when suddenly the front door swung open. All I heard was, 'La, la, la, la, la.' In skipped a freckle-faced, as tapped as a sink, girl. She looked around and walked over towards us, looked down and walked back. 'And don't come back again,' I screamed. I don't think she heard me. Obviously not since she walked back over with a spoon.

I saw her looking down at my dad licking her lips. She pulled back her arm and took a giant spoonful out of my dad then she ate it. She spat it out, stuck out her tongue and waved her arm about in front of it. (Told you she was tapped.) Then she walked over to my mum and did exactly the same, this time without any of the mad waving. And then there was me, she pulled back her arm with the spoon in her hand, took one big spoonful and swallowed me whole.

That was the end of me. Don't ask me how I'm telling the story, that's for consulting with my agent.

Drew Evans (12)
Kirkby College, Nottingham

A Holiday To Remember
(An extract)

A girl with a pretty face, no blemishes and long golden curls cascading down past her shoulders brandished a long pink sword, stabbed the terrifying, evil dragon straight through his heart. She stepped back as the dragon swayed and fell with a thud length-long in front of her. She threw back her head and gave a victorious, triumphant laugh, then she stepped on top of the dead dragon in her stiletto shoes and shouted, 'You are rid of the fearsome dragon!'

Then a voice from behind her called loudly, 'Wake up, we're here! *Wake* up!'

The girl slowly opened her eyes and stared around her surroundings, she was in a car and her little sister was shaking her vigorously. 'Come on, time to get up lazy bones!'

'Another dream again!' sighed the girl as she climbed out of the car and stepped into Cornwall. She was looking at the floor. It was covered in daisies. She felt somehow magical standing on them, it seemed just like a dream. She looked up and in front of her was something that looked like a castle, that was towering above her, it was just like a fairy tale!

The door suddenly swung back with a bang and a butler stood in the doorway, 'Are you going to enter, Miss Green?' asked a hoarse, raspy voice from the butler.

How did he know my name? thought the girl and started to walk through the door into a big hall with a ceiling over 20 feet high! She turned around to ask the butler how he knew her name, but he was gone. She ran outside again and saw her parents unloading the car and her sister glued to the car TV (her favourite programme was on), everything seemed normal.

'Come and help us unpack, Paprika, dear,' called her mother from inside the boot.

'Wait a minute Mum,' replied the girl. Paprika turned around to look at the castle-like building but there was only a cottage there. She walked up to the cottage and then looked down at the ground. *Where is the castle-like building and where are the daisies?* Paprika wondered to herself as she ran back to the car to help her parents unload their things.

'Is the cottage nice?' asked her father.

'I don't know, I have not been inside,' replied Paprika taking her suitcase from the boot.

'Don't be silly of course, you have, I saw you go in earlier!'

'Oh yeah, erm, it was, erm, really nice,' lied Paprika. If she told her family about walking into a castle they would think she was a loony! She reached into the boot again to pull out another suitcase then ran off shouting, 'I bags best room!'

'That's not fair! Wait for me!' her sister screamed leaping out of the car but Paprika was already inside the house searching for the best rooms.

Paprika found a lovely room which she thought was absolutely perfect! The room had pink walls with a purple border around them. On the walls were shelves, there was a wardrobe, even a TV and a computer but best of all in the middle of the room was a king-sized bed. It looked so springy and perfect for bouncing on so she took 5 steps back and then she started to run forwards and leapt, ready to land on the bouncy bed, but she landed smack on the floor with a thud!

After about one minute of being dazed from such a heavy crash she slowly opened her eyes to reveal a dingy, horrible room, all there was inside the room was a single bed in the corner and a crooked shelf above, the walls were mouldy green and grey colours. It was awful and, as Paprika sat on the floor, the more she began to realise what had happened, it was just like the castle. She stood up slowly and shuffled over towards the grotty bed, she sat on it depressed …

Alice Thoburn (12)
Kirkby College, Nottingham

Lucy And Her Curiosity

Lucy wasn't afraid of anything and that's what got her into trouble so much she was always very curious. Lucy had long brown hair usually tied into a scruffy ponytail at the back. She didn't really care about her appearance, she always seemed to saunter along by herself watching everyone else to see if she could find something interesting to involve herself in.

It was a Monday afternoon and Lucy was walking past the school gates, her bag dragging on the floor behind her when she noticed something interesting, there was a piece of paper on the floor, everyone was stepping on it not noticing anything, but Lucy could just about figure out a red cross marked in the corner of the page. She picked it up and found that it was a treasure map. She followed the treasure map's directions for miles and miles keeping her eyes fixed to it.

After around 2 hours had passed she came to an island surrounded by water. The sun dazzled on its golden, fine sand. It was deserted except for a palm tree. Lucy walked over to the palm tree to get some shade, she was about to sit down but instead fell into a hole which had appeared from nowhere. Lucy gushed down and realised she was in the sea, an old shipwreck, which was … shark-infested! Her foot had got caught on a rope with only enough to reach the surface. Her heart was pounding. Would she live … or not?

Anna Robinson (12)
Leicester High School for Girls, Leicester

The Frightening Metro

My legs were wobbling when I walked down a few steps to reach the London Underground. We went swiftly down the enormous elevators, there were lots of them, all of them creeping up and then crawling down again. I nervously held my ticket against a hole. Then suddenly it snatched it away from me.

There were thousands of people waiting around anxiously for their train to collect them. There were lots of businessmen rushing around like little ants trying to escape. There were also lots of foreigners wandering around cluelessly, wondering where to go.

On the platform I stood shocked, but the thing that shocked me the most were the gloomy, dirty, dark, dingy tunnels which stood both sides of me. I started to get scared when the low rumblings of something started to emerge from one tunnel. It started getting louder until there were two bright, gleaming lights staring out of one tunnel. A train pulled up and everyone scrambled onto it.

My hands gripped tightly onto the handrail. Then with a sudden jolt the train started to move until it was in complete darkness. It started to get a bit faster until the carriage was wobbling from side to side. My hands were sweating now and my face was just like a cherry. The train came to a sudden halt and the doors opened. We got off and a few minutes later we were in broad daylight. Then I couldn't wait to go on it again!

Emma Boyd (11)
Leicester High School for Girls, Leicester

Why Do We Hick Up And Not Down?

Over years people have wondered why we hick up and not down and this is the answer ...

Many years ago there lived Princess Maria. But although she searched high and low she could not find 'Mr Right'. One day her father warned her that she must leave soon.

One night when she was dreaming of her man, an angel appeared to her, telling her that he did exist and that she could find him locked up in a castle up on Mount Hick. Now the princess knew that this was a dangerous journey to Mount Hick but she knew that she could manage it. And so she set off the next day.

On the way she was greeted by many monsters, including many sighing flies, telling her what she already knew, 'She'll never do this, she'll never find him.'

And when she came to a castle she ran in and started to climb the stairs and never noticed her aching legs, she was so eager for him. And he was there, with his arms out, waiting to meet her.

'Princess Maria, I thought you would never come.'

She was surprised because it were as if they had known each other forever. She did a small gasp, and another, she couldn't help it, there were funny little noises coming with the gasps. The only thing that could stop her was a kiss from the prince. And whenever she thought of her journey, up Hick she started to 'hick up'.

Susanna Goodhart (11)
Leicester High School for Girls, Leicester

The Story Of The Ghost Of Leicester High!

'The door slammed behind her! She was trapped! There was a deadly smell! She looked round for an explanation but all she could see was a flickering streetlight through the barred windows! She tried to open the door but it was jammed! Some people say she was left in there until one day she died and still wasn't found by anyone! Some say it is just a silly ghost story. The truth we will probably never know!'

'Wow, what an amazing story! It's so scary! I'm getting shivers just thinking about what the truth could be! I guess, like you said though, we will never know the truth about poor, innocent Lucy Jennings!'

Suddenly Laura's pencil case dropped to the floor!

'I'll tell you one thing, even if there was never a Lucy Jennings, there was Mrs Powell. You know the one!' Laura told Jenny.

'Of course! The ghost of the old head teacher of Leicester High. I can't actually believe I didn't think of her! My big sister told me that she actually saw her! Once she was going back into school as she had forgotten her maths book; there was no one there apart from her! That was what it felt like anyway! But although she didn't know, someone was watching her! She heard a sweeping noise and turned round, there was no one there! That was when she saw her. She ran home and didn't look back! It will haunt her for the rest of her life!'

Rebecca Twynham (12)
Leicester High School for Girls, Leicester

The Hallowe'en That I Will Never Forget

It was a dark and stormy night but that didn't stop anyone from trick or treating. It was Hallowe'en and as usual me and the rest of the Cool Crew had gone out on our rounds.

The Thompson's house was unusually decorated with pumpkins and *Beware* signs. As a joke we decided to host a break-in. We all crept around the back and looked for some stones to throw at the windows.

Suddenly we jumped as we heard a creaking noise but realised it was a cat. A black cat.

First, Hannah went through the window. She checked if the coast was clear and then helped everyone else through. I went last.

Once we were all through we wandered around seeing if there was a light switch anywhere. Tom leaned back and suddenly the light flickered and switched on.

We all opened our mouths in amazement as if something was stuck in our throats; the room had cobwebs in every corner of the ceiling and it was dusty everywhere we looked.

Just then Liz pointed to a picture which we were all very certain was a ghost. We all looked at each other and I was sure we were all thinking the same thing. The house was haunted!

I looked at the windows. Suddenly the pieces of glass came together like a puzzle, to form a brand new window. We heard a gruesome laugh, 'Ha, ha, ha …'

Sonal Shah (11)
Leicester High School for Girls, Leicester

Demon Siege

It was tranquil in the cloud-sheltered mountains of the Himalayas. All around there was a deafening silence that had been so for many a century. Then a faint drumbeat was heard. Gradually it began to echo across the mountains, gathering like a dark shadow in the night, twisting and binding, swallowing anything it touched and draping the hills in a nocturnal wonderland.

Located in a serene area of one of the Himalayas' mighty peaks lay a small temple. It was neither grand nor magnificent but its presence was clearly felt. Any animals living on the mountain flocked to it as if it contained some kind of peaceful essence, which was irresistible to any creature. Inside this temple lived an order of legendary Buddhist monks. The Shaolin Monks. Masters of the martial arts, with unbreakable spirits and iron wills. They were the best.

The drum was growing louder now. Birds were starting to flock away and animals were retreating to their homes. In the distance a cry could be heard. It was getting closer. It was clearer now. A feral chant was being bellowed out by what sounded like an army of wolves shattering the serene atmosphere like glass.

In the temple the Shaolin monks in their traditional dress of orange tunics and black belts heard an alarmed cry of fear from the lookout. The monks ran out from their dormitories and meditation chambers to hear what was the trouble. The lookout uttered but one petrified word, 'Demons ...'

Joshua Taylor (13)
Ludlow CE School, Ludlow

The Valley

The dark expanse of forest loomed above the frozen stream. Despite light snowfall the trees were a dark green, stripped of their white coat by a biting wind.

Few plants could find the strength to force their way through the hard, frost-covered patch of bare earth by the frozen water. Beneath the thick ice nothing stirred. If there had been anything alive in that cold water before the harsh winter it was long gone now.

Bleak, desolate mountains towered above the solitary valley; white shapes against an equally white sky. A few flakes of snow drifted down from the expanse of clouds. More fell, until nothing could be seen apart from the ground beneath your feet. The delicate flakes twirled and drifted, creating an illusion of dark shapes across the ice and in the forest, always moving before they could be seen fully.

The almost deafening silence was only broken by the rush of the wind and, occasionally, a wolf howl - sometimes close by, sometimes further away, sometimes sounding as if it came from the very mountains themselves.

Eventually, when the snow settles, nothing is as it was before. It is like being transported to another place, another *world*. Any colour is gone, covered by the unrelenting whiteness. The dark green of the forest had disappeared, covered by a screen, a colourless but intriguing barrier, that blanks the mind and numbs the body, waiting to catch you out and lead you to a cold, frozen grave.

Hugh Williamson (13)
Ludlow CE School, Ludlow

I'm Scared …

It kills me to open my eyes. It kills me to watch. Instead, I hide away, somewhere dark, wrap my arms around my knees and I pray for the screaming to stop - it never does.

I'm scared. I'm always crying. I don't have any friends. The only real thing I know is the darkness between the four walls of my closet.

Mummy was raped today. She doesn't know I know, but I know. There are a lot of things that I'm not supposed to know, or tell anybody, like why Mummy's bleeding, or why she has no face.

I think Mummy's dead. I haven't heard her in so long, and there's a smell coming from downstairs. I think Daddy killed her, and now he's going to kill me.

I suppose it's my fault, everything. I got Daddy mad, and he hit me. I was alright though, I didn't feel a thing. But Mummy and Daddy weren't, they shouted, and argued, and fought a lot after that.

I got confused while my daddy was on the phone, I heard him shouting at someone. I heard him mention me. He said he had no son any more. I got that scary feeling again, of emptiness, I've had it since that day Daddy got mad, like I wasn't really here.

I got brave today. I was going to turn on the light. So, I reached for the cord and pulled. But as soon as it came on, I turned it off. Someone was in here with me, and he looked just like me, but, he wasn't moving - not an inch. Just as if, he were me, but frozen, and red, and like I was not, empty, and white.

Help me.

I'm scared …

Kieran Vyas (13)
Manor High School, Leicester

What Lies Beneath?

The moon was covered by never-ending clouds and the many overgrown bushes didn't help my imagination. I cursed myself for making such a noise. No one could know that I was here. I had to find out.

The wind smacked the remaining walls and I shivered. The thin T-shirt and jeans I had on gave me little warmth.

Suddenly, I felt something brush against my back. I spun around, expecting the worst, and saw an exotic bird peering at me from behind the ghostly outline of a towering tree.

I picked up a brick and tossed it aside. The ground underneath was covered with damp soil so that, as I clawed my way through the damp earth, bits of soil clogged my fingernails. Gradually, my hands got deeper and deeper into the earth until they hit something hard. I drew my hands out quickly and stared at the thing that I had discovered. It was a shoebox. Carefully, I pulled it out and gazed at the decoration on it. There were gorgeous beads of different colours and pictures of the same group of young girls, who were smiling and laughing. I opened the lid and saw, to my surprise, nothing. The box was full of dirt and the paper on the sides had been torn, as if whatever had been in there had been taken out quickly. All of a sudden a gush of wind came from nowhere and, as I spun round, the bird came hurtling towards me.

Charlotte Fox (13)
Manor High School, Leicester

You Must Live!

I stepped through the door and all was quiet, maybe too quiet.

'Mum? Dad?' I said, no one answered. *They might be out,* I thought and went to get a drink of Coke and something to eat and then it happened ... two people smashed through the kitchen window and knocked into me. I fell to the ground with a thud. Carefully I stood up and looked around. The weird people, a man and a woman, were there standing by the worktop.

'What do you want?' I whispered, scared for my life.

'We are taking you into care. You must come with us and we must hurry before they come.' He looked around concerned and then looked back at me.

'But why do we have to go? What about my life? What about my parents?'

The man looked at me, then spoke to the woman. 'Should we tell her? She has a right to know, after all they were her parents.'

'Alright then. Narisha your ...'

'How do you know my name?' I was so scared and confused but I wanted to know what was happening.

'Never mind now. Your parents they're ... they're ... they're dead! They were killed by these people. Your parents were spies and were killed by the enemy. The Germans!'

'No ... they can't have they have just gone to the corner shop probably. They aren't dead!'

'They are! I'm sorry but we have to go before they come to kill you! They must never kill you! You must live!'

Narisha Vora (13)
Manor High School, Leicester

A Day In The Life Of A Martian

Gurkulas-Jimthy-Harin or Gurk for short, woke up in his rest pouch, groaned, rolled over and went back to sleep again. After another two hours of beautiful rest he awoke to see his floating clock proclaiming that he was already half an hour late for work.

Swearing, Gurk struggled into his earth-print kimono and moon boots, grabbed his canvas collector's bag and gulped down some grizzen juice as he ran down the road to the nearest lift which would take him out of Zacatrice City and onto the scarlet deserts of Mars. Gurk was a collector. He would search the sands of the red planet to try and find blue rubies, the most valuable in the galaxy. Gurk wasn't very lucky. The closest to valuable Gurk had got was through a rusty old Earth probe called 'Beagle Two' which gave him enough cash to pay the bills for a month but nothing more. Gurk's lunch was a simple grizzen juice and a sandy sandwich. Yuck.

It was nearing the end of the day and Gurk was hot, dusty and … hang on! He saw something glinting through the sand, something big and blue! He dug and dug and gasped to see that he had unearthed a blue ruby the size of his head!

That night, Gurk was the legend of all the collectors (having to buy drinks all round of course!). But one thing was for certain, he could move out of his tiny flat now!

Rebecca Tobin (13)
Manor High School, Leicester

My Dad!
(For my lovely father)

Now what can I say about my dad? He is the best, the funniest, the coolest and the busiest person in the whole wide universe. Somehow, my chirpy father is a doctor.

As I pace through the front door, it is very quiet. I mean you could literally hear a pin drop and even that would have caused a shock. I listened vigilantly and could hear clicks and clacks. OK, so my father was on the computer. I walked into the computer room with a humongous smile on my face. Dad greeted me with an even bigger smile. That was our joke, if I do something really wacky; my dad tries to do something even wackier. Yep, my dad was unquestionably in a good mood, alright! I took a quick glimpse of the computer and noticed that Dad was doing a presentation about Parkinson's Disease and strokes. The presentation included the history, the facts and figures and the people involved in it.

I remember that once Dad told me about his job as a doctor. Dad is a physician, he treats elderly people. He told me that his day starts a bit like this ...

'When I reach the hospital, I check-in, meet my patients, have a meeting with other doctors, have lunch, head for a presentation, come home and ... cuddle you to bits.'

Yuck! Dad had spoilt the finale. I mean it wasn't as if I were a tomboy, but there had to be a limit. Anyway, from that day onwards - my dad has been my role model.

Charu Thanvi (13)
Manor High School, Leicester

The Soldier

I shot up from the dark, underground, grubby trench. The first of the bombs blasted rapidly. The chilly breeze swept my pale, uncomfortable face. I was alone, frightened with this act of war. Waiting, waiting, I lay waiting for my turn. The sight of death taunted me as millions lay shot dead. The constant barraging gave us no peace. A fear of death quivered up my spine.

'Next section!' ordered our cantankerous general.

I slithered out carefully and peered cautiously onto no-man's-land. I held the rifle tightly. I closed my eyes slowly and thought of my mum's sweet smell of home-made buns and my girlfriend's warm loving hugs.

Suddenly I was pushed down hard onto the muddy ground. I pulled the trigger with strength and hope. Struggling up, the fragile dead surrounded me. Blood flooded the area. A blur stood in front of me, innocent people rushing in every direction.

With all my might, I shot my last bullet. It hit. It hit a young German soldier. He looked very like my friend, Sam, from home.

I remember the days, when my dad told me about his old, kind German friend, Franz. He was helpful and kind. Guilt overwhelmed me about what I had done. A horrible feeling shuddered in my lonely soul.

Sonam Mehta (13)
Manor High School, Leicester

A Danger To Sophia Harrington

Whilst the sweet birds were chirping harmoniously in the evergreen trees, the sound of summer woke me up, as I was in a feeling of warm relaxation. Thinking it was going to be a fine day where I could just nip down to the swimming baths and have a sensational rest in the bubbling jacuzzi was a total mistake.

The instant I dipped my feet into the water, I jumped back in astonishment and shock! The water was ice-cold! As I fumbled around, I felt a hand groping around my ankles, a cold, slithery hand. It was crawling up my leg like a slow, monstrous beast, maybe even a tarantula.

I screamed with all my might and let out a yell of terror. The whole area was deserted; I was isolated with this brute coming towards me, more and more every second. The pool went dark and gloomy; I could not see a thing. Rapidly, I felt as if all my life were flashing before my eyes, and I was fading away into doom. All I could see was a colossal shadow of a mighty fiend towering over me. I felt a tinge of pain in my neck and within three seconds, blood was gushing down my arm and my body, rustling like the strong wind on a stormy, thunderous day. The feeling of fear spread over me. I screamed. Then nothing. Blackness.

Karishma Manji (13)
Manor High School, Leicester

Hell's Grasp

The shivering wind howled through the transparent, coloured windows of the old ruined church. The whole building had collapsed during the disastrous earthquake a couple of weeks before. In actual fact, I'm lucky to even have lived! People say it was caused by a deathly ghost - *Mary!* It was told that ever since she was found out to be a ghost, she had been haunting this village high and low ...

As I stepped cautiously into the ancient church, whispering sounds aroused the surroundings. A shiver swept me off my feet as I froze in horror. A sharp whistle streamed through the air like a bullet from a shotgun. I was absolutely terrified. Frozen to the spot. What was going on? What should I do? Everything was happening so quickly. Suddenly, a gush of wind sent a shock down my spine as I instantly jolted upright. My vision blurred as I spun round helplessly. A ghastly white blur flashed before my eyes. I felt waves of agony down my back, killing me every second. I tried to fight whatever came in my path but Hell's hand had me in its clutch.

Shadowy figures swarmed through my brain. I had lost total control of my mind and body. Then, complete darkness apart from a fragile light at the back of my mind. I desperately grabbed for the blinding light, in hope to have my life back. Deep in my unconscious thoughts, I could hear the sound of a siren ...

Shreena Sonecha (13)
Manor High School, Leicester

The Woman

One chilling winter's twilight, we sat by the crackling fireplace in our home. We lived in a lovely mansion, in Bern. We bought the ancient home unknowingly. It was this night we found out the disturbing secret of our haunted mansion.

I slept, that night, like a baby, but my dreams weren't as innocent. It was in our home. There was a woman I had never seen before; she was young with silky blonde hair and blue eyes. I was following her, but the closer I got to her, the further away she ran. She started crying and panicking. It was like she was running away from me, like I was a monster. I was uncontrollable. I cornered her, drew my bloody knife, and stabbed her! She died instantly. Suddenly I woke. Beads of sweat were rolling down my forehead.

The following evening, we sat by the fireplace when unexpectedly the lights went out! We were left in total darkness and went to open the curtains to let in some light. She was standing there! As pale as flour, glaring intensely at us.

She advanced dangerously, as we retreated. She had walked straight through the window. Now she was wearing an evil grin. Her mouth was surrounded with blood, and she was carrying a dripping knife. I looked around frantically. The rest of my family had been slaughtered! Her extended arms, her grin grew terrifyingly. I felt a sharp pain. My life flashed before my eyes. Then, I felt nothing.

Durga Gandhi (13)
Manor High School, Leicester

Untitled

An ice-cold wind passed over Sara like a piercing whip. A shiver shot down the twenty-one year-old, causing the hairs on the back of her neck to stand on end. Sara carried on walking through the wilderness, determined to seek her goal, forcing herself against the wind which was now forming some kind of preventative barrier disallowing her to venture forward. The clock of darkness had been set to pitch-black and Sara was unaware how long she had been walking for, or why she was even there in the first place. Somehow this had not bothered her, the thought of reaching sanctuary was more important than the loss of her memory.

Suddenly she stopped, listening intently. Among the wind and the sound of her own rapid breathing, there was another resonance; the voice of a child singing. Though the world in which Sara had unintentionally entered appeared deserted, it was definitely there. Slowly but surely, the echoing sound was mounting steadily. Abruptly it stopped, as at that moment a shot of pain struck up Sara like a lightning bolt causing her to fall to the floor contorted in pain. The air from her lungs was sucked away as she tried gasping heavily for breath. She looked up, trying to work out what had caused this intense pain. The sight that hit her was far worse than what she'd prepared herself for. The pitch-black wasteland had now been lit up with bright white lights. A sudden wave of horror passed over her when the truth dawned. These lights were people, well at least they used to be. They were dead. Ghostly transparent, Victorian children were playing skipping games and riding around on floating bicycles that rose no higher than two inches off the ground. This was the Land of the Dead that Sara had inadvertently walked into, unless ... no, she couldn't be ... not *dead*.

At that moment an icy hand clasped Sara's shoulder causing her body temperature to drop instantly. The singing started again, this time louder and eerier, piercing the air and making the sweat on Sara's forehead freeze somehow. She could sense her shoulder turning white. The icy feeling spread through her body and as her bones started splitting as they froze. Sara was paralysed in fear; she was frozen to the ground, unable to do anything. The singing stopped as suddenly as it had started. The singing girl suddenly spoke in a harsh, intimidating voice, 'This is Samhaim, the World of the Dead.'

Jemma Healey (13)
Manor High School, Leicester

Sam And Trarminda - The Best Friends In Town

Once upon a time there was an ogre called Sam. When he was walking down the street he saw Tom and Jerry running away. Sam said, 'Stop!' but Tom and Jerry kept on running from a dragon called Trarminda. The dragon was in town and was scaring people. Trarminda was trying to catch the people. He was flying and chasing after the people and grabbing them by their heads. Trarminda didn't realise that he was scaring people, he thought he was making friends but he wasn't. Sam saw the dragon and ran after it and chased him up to the mountains. The mountains were like volcanoes, they were very big and steep. Sam felt mad because Trarminda was scaring his friends.

Sam got the dragon's tail and spun it around and around until the dragon got dizzy. The dragon said, 'Stop I don't like that, all I want is a friend.'

Sam said, 'Sorry! I want a friend too.'

Trarminda and Sam went back to the town. All the people ran away. Tom and Jerry were scared but Sam said, 'Stop! Don't be afraid Trarminda just wants to be a friend.' Tom and Jerry forgave Trarminda.

Sam, Tom, Jerry and Trarminda lived happily ever after. It took a little time for the people of the town to forgive Trarminda for scaring them but they eventually loved him and looked after him. They let him live in the town with them.

Tim Riches (14)
Maplewell Hall Special School, Loughborough

The Disaster

It was a cold December morning. As Amy stirred, she felt something on her bed, it was her dog Toby. As she started to get up he moved. She got dressed then looked at the clock, she was late for school. Then she ran downstairs, her mum was making breakfast, she saw her coming. 'Good morning,' said Mum.

'Good morning,' said Amy. 'I'm late for school.'

Rob her brother was ready to go, he called to Amy, 'Are you ready to go? It's pet day today.'

'Let's take Toby to school,' said Amy.

'Good idea,' said Rob.

'Let's go then,' said Amy. They walked out of the door, 'Bye Mum,' they said.

They got there just in time for the bell. James and Anna were waiting for them with their dog Buster. He is a friend of Toby's, they always went to the park together. They lined up then went into school, their teacher Mrs Baker led them into their classroom. 'Sit down class, it's pet day today.' Amy tied Toby's lead to her hand, Anna did the same with Buster. 'Good morning class,' said Mrs Baker.

Everyone had brought their pets in. Billy brought his rat in, Jamie brought his guinea pig called Zack, Aaron brought his snake in. Sammie brought her fish in and Jo brought her cat in. 'Mrs Baker are we allowed to get our animals out to show?' said Aaron.

'Yes, in a minute, I have got to do the register first,' said Mrs Baker. 'James?' said Mrs Baker.

'Yes Mrs Baker.'

'Anna?'

'Yes Mrs Baker.'

'Jo?'

'Yes Mrs Baker.'

'Billy?'

'Yes Mrs Baker.'

'Jamie?'

'Yes Mrs Baker.'

She'd soon finished the register. Jo opened the cat cage, the cat ran across the room, everyone jumped out of their seats. Toby and Buster ran after the cat.

'Come back,' shouted Rob and James, Toby and Buster were just running out of the door when someone stopped them, it was the headmaster, Mr Hamming.

'What is going on in here?' shouted Mr Hamming. 'Who is the cause of this mayhem?' Amy and Rob came forward, so did Anna and James. 'You four with me now, get in,' he said.

Their parents were called, they came straight away. They got grounded for a month, they were only allowed out of the house for school.

Helen Edwards (13)
Maplewell Hall Special School, Loughborough

Scary School

It was getting late and Steven and James were going to Mr Furborough's classroom to do some work, and they were walking on the grass. Then he saw a ghost. It looked like the ghost of Mr Ginger Neal. They both shouted, 'Argh ... !'

It was blue and they could see right through it. They jumped over a bush then ran towards a classroom door. They burst through the door and inside it was scary, dull and there were cobwebs in the corners. It was like an old prison. Steven and James felt very scared. All of a sudden the ghost of Mr Neal started to bang on the front door. James screamed and started to shake. Steven's teeth began to chatter and his hair began to go grey. They thought they would never escape but Mr Neal smashed through the front door to catch Steven and James. They hid behind the door and then ran past Mr Neal and locked the front door leaving him inside.

'Let's go!' gasped James with a sigh of relief.

'Good idea,' replied Steven.

Rhona McLean (15)
Maplewell Hall Special School, Loughborough

Tom And Jerry And The Island

My name is Tom and I was on a ship with my friend Jerry, then pirates came. They took us hostage. In the middle of the sea they pushed us overboard. Before they pushed us we put a letter on a bird and then they pushed us off. We held our breath and fell in the water. A dolphin came and helped us to shore.

When we got to shore we found we were in Neverland where Peter Pan lived with the Lost Boys. We found the children and played games. When we were tired we sat down around a fire and talked about what had happened with the pirates. The boys thought it might have been Captain Hook. They got their weapons and went to fight him that night. I went with Jerry to help but Jerry got hurt whilst fighting the captain. After a long fight the Lost Boys won and the pirates ran away.

We had to carry Jerry back to the camp and Tinkerbell made him well again. We went to sleep and I woke up in the morning in my own bed. I heard Mum calling me, 'Wake up, time for school!' I realised it was only a dream. I felt happy but a bit sad because it was good with the Lost Boys. I hope I go back soon.

Robert Shirton (14)
Maplewell Hall Special School, Loughborough

Day At School

There were two girls called Lisa and her best friend, Samantha. Lisa was tall with lovely blue eyes, had brown hair in two ponytails and was wearing a blue top and jeans. Samantha had blue eyes like Lisa, she had her hair down with a pretty clip in and was wearing a pink top and skirt, and was a bit small.

This is how the story goes. It was a boring Monday at school and Lisa and Samantha were in the playground talking about what they'd done at the weekend until the bell went for lining up time. Their teacher came and went into the classroom but Lisa walked straight into a lovely boy who said, 'Watch where you are going next time, I nearly went flying flat on my face,' he said crossly.

'Sorry I didn't mean to,' Lisa said worriedly, so off Lisa went to class.

She was sitting next to Lauren and Samantha when their teacher was taking the register. Then Lisa said, 'Can I take the register back please?'

'Yes you can,' said the teacher.

When Lisa took the register back she bumped into the lovely boy again. 'Oh no, not you again,' said the boy.

'Hi, sorry again about what happened before class,' Lisa said.

'That's OK and by the way my name is Tom,' he said shyly.

'I'll see you at break time then,' Lisa said, so back to class she went.

It was break time and Lisa, Samantha and Lauren were all playing a game called 'Haunted House' and in the middle of the game Lisa saw Tom again. 'Can you come here for a minute or two please?' said Tom.

'Yes I can and my name is Lisa by the way,' she said.

'I know I bumped into you this morning, but I thought to myself, would you like to be friends with me?'

'Yes, that would be lovely and do you want to play with us lot because we're playing Haunted House?' Lisa said.

'OK,' Tom said.

So off they went to play Haunted House and had a great time.

Lisa James (16)
Maplewell Hall Special School, Loughborough

The Last Dragon

One day there were four animals who were friends, they were Boris the hedgehog, Freddy the fox, Amy the rabbit and Nick the ferret. They were playing one day and were talking about a dragon in the mountains, he was called Scorch, he was the last dragon on Earth. Scorch was a very angry dragon because he was lonely. Boris, Freddy, Amy and Nick decided to go and find Scorch and be his friend.

It was sunny when they left, they walked for miles before they found they had to cross a big river, they managed to swim across. They were then wet and cold so they built a fire to get warm.

The next day they went to find Scorch in a cave where they had seen smoke coming out. Amy got very scared but Boris said, 'Don't be afraid, I'll protect you.'

They crept into the cave and Scorch heard them and tried to kill them. He tried to use fire but because he was a young dragon he didn't know how and instead he sneezed and smoke came out! Boris said, 'Yuck,' and all the children laughed.

Scorch got angry and roared, 'Get out of my cave!'

Amy said, 'OK,' and ran! Boris went to find Amy. Nick and Freddy stayed and tried to calm Scorch down, they gave him meat because it was his favourite food. Scorch started to be friendly and trusted the animals, he said that they could come back and play whenever they wanted. So now every year the animals go back to see Scorch and he wasn't angry or lonely any more.

Sian Palmer (14)
Maplewell Hall Special School, Loughborough

The Dragon Crystal

Once upon a time some dragons lived in a field where it was peaceful and quiet. The dragons were all different colours and were very beautiful. A magic crystal used to keep them alive. The crystal was safe in a tower. It used to shine light onto the field to keep the dragons alive. The leader of the dragons was called Dracin, he was big and tough and a very kind of dragon.

One day Dracin stood before the dragons and told them some bad news, 'Somebody has stolen the crystal and unless we find it, in two days we will die.' The dragons felt very weak, tired and sad. Dracin decided to find the crystal, he thought that Sly, the dark dragon, had stolen the crystal and had taken it to the Dark Castle in the forest. Leon the unicorn was friends with Dracin and he said he would help. Dracin and Leon left the field, the other dragons felt very sad as they thought they might never see Dracin again.

They arrived at the Dark Castle and Dracin could see the crystal in the Black Tower. They flew over the tower and found a door. Leon used his horn to bash the door open. They took the crystal and tried to escape, just as Sly flew down. Dracin dropped the crystal, Sly grabbed it and Dracin challenged Sly to a fight. They flew backwards and forwards in the sky blowing fireballs at each other and scratching and biting. Eventually Dracin won as he refused to give up and Sly was very tired and weak.

Dracin and Leon left the castle to return home and put the crystal back. All the dragons had a huge party to celebrate their return.

Charlotte King (14)
Maplewell Hall Special School, Loughborough

The Haunted School

One day Jack and Ryan went to the park late at night to meet some friends. When they got to the park no one was there. Suddenly they saw a light at the school. 'Let's go and see what that light is,' said Jack.

When they got closer it looked like a prison and it was very dark.

Jack said, 'It's so creepy let's go.'

'You don't know what will happen?'

'Never mind let's go, it looks like a prison.' The weather was so bad, it was thundering and raining.

Ryan said, 'Let's go into the school.'

They went into the school because someone told them there was a key that opened all the doors. It was so cold and really dark, they went upstairs to see who was up there.

'There isn't any one, we will try and find the key.'

They went upstairs and Jack was frightened because it was like a prison. There were bars on the windows and a chill in the air. Jack shivered and goosebumps came up on his arm.

They went into this room and they saw the key. Ryan went to get it but someone was coming up the stairs. Ryan and Jack hid in the cupboard and someone came and looked in the room. He went and locked the door. Jack and Ryan were scared and the man took the key with him. They were stuck in that room till the next day. Jack was scared. The room was haunted, Jack saw shadows at the windows. Ryan saw a ghost 'What do you want?' The ghost did not say anything and the ghost went but Jack did not know where the ghost had gone.

Then the next morning a man came and unlocked the door and put the key back. Jack and Ryan ran out of the room and looked around the school.

Jack saw a phone and he went to ring his mum but the phone was not working. 'Let's try and get out of this school.' Quickly they ran down the stairs. They went to go out of the front door but it was locked and Jack said, 'Let's go and get the key and it will let us out of the school.'

Daniel Newbold (15)
Maplewell Hall Special School, Loughborough

The Dark Woods

Sid and Fred were playing football in the park. As it started to get dark the wind started to blow. Sid and Fred decided to play dares in the woods, as they had been hearing stories about the woods at school. They heard that this beast lived in the woods. Then they were arguing about who would go into the woods first so they both decided to go in there together. Then they heard the noises. The noises were a big bear in the woods. It was growling and snarling. Sid and Fred were scared and the bear got them both cornered. The bear was still growling and snarling at Sid and Fred. They were scared but Sid had a plan ...

He sharpened some sticks with a piece of slate and the bear was getting closer. Then Sid plucked up his courage and stabbed the bear right in its heart. Then the bear fell to its feet. The bear died in a big puddle of blood and Sid and Fred were free.

Khan Dean (15)
Maplewell Hall Special School, Loughborough

The Dark Dungeon

It was getting dark and Kirk and James were playing football, when James kicked the ball over a wall. James climbed over to get the ball and then shouted to Kirk that he couldn't find it. Kirk said, 'I'll be there in a minute,' then he too climbed over and met up with James. They found the ball. Then they looked up ...

They saw this huge house. It looked dark and scary. Kirk and James thought they could see someone looking out of the window. It looked like a boy about their own age. 'Shall we find out who he is?' asked Kirk.

'OK, it will be fun to go inside,' replied James.

They crept through the door and inside they saw the boy go through another door. Kirk and James followed. They went down some worn steps into a dungeon. It was cold, damp and spooky and smelt of blood and dead people; a sweet sickly smell that caught the very depth of their noses.

All of a sudden the noise of a high-pitched motor split the silence. It was a chainsaw. Kirk ran but the chainsaw was swung and tore through Kirk's leg. Kirk's blood-curdling scream echoed through the building. James ran to help Kirk but the chainsaw was swung again and took James' leg off just above the knee. The single light shone through a red mist as blood was splattered into the air. James opened his mouth to scream but no sound came from him, so he just lay there with a look of death on his face.

They thought they would never escape but once they had come to their senses, the boys looked round and saw several bones on the dungeon floor. They picked up two of the longest ones and used them as supports to hobble out of the dungeon. Luckily they were not followed. James gasped with a sigh of relief. 'Let's hop it,' laughed Kirk.

Kirk Baker (15)
Maplewell Hall Special School, Loughborough

Haunted Castle

It was getting late and Luke and Frazer were going to visit the castle as they wanted to see what it was like inside. Luke and Frazer walked up the stony path. Then they saw the castle. It looked old and big. It was made of stone and it was dark and mysterious. Luke and Frazer went closer to the castle and then they saw something huge and hairy.

'Is that what I think it is?' asked Luke.

'Yes it is,' replied Frazer, 'it's a spider.'

They crept through the door and inside they looked around the castle for food. They went upstairs and found an attic. They didn't find any food but they found more spiders. It was like a carpet of spiders. It was cold and scary.

All of a sudden the spiders found a hole in the floor and all went down it. Luke and Frazer ran out of the attic and saw all the spiders fall in a fire underneath the attic and burn.

Luke and Frazer ran out of the front door and ran down the path. The children started to run back home. 'We're lucky to be alive,' gasped Luke.

'Thank God,' replied Frazer.

Lana Riches (15)
Maplewell Hall Special School, Loughborough

The Wicked Wizard

One day there was some children playing football in the garden, they were called Tommy, Roger and Jill. Suddenly there was a big man at the gate, he grabbed the children and put them in a blue van and took them to a cottage in the countryside. The man wanted the children to use in his magic spells, the man was a wizard. The wizard locked them in a cage in the cellar and gave the children rabbit stew to eat. The children were very upset, especially Jill. Tommy said, 'Let's try and escape.' Tommy had grabbed the wizard's keys from his pocket as he was carrying the children. They had to be quick because they didn't want the wizard to come and look for his keys.

They managed to climb down from the cage and ran through a passage which took them to where the wizard did all his spells. Tommy knew about magic and they made a potion which exploded and made a hole in the wall. The children escaped through the hole as the wizard was coming into the room to see what the noise was. The wizard was angry and chased the children but they were ready to catch him. They threw a net over him and locked him in the cellar with his keys. Tommy had a mobile phone and he rang the police who came and locked the wizard away forever, and took the children back home where they were safe.

Alix Moore (12)
Maplewell Hall Special School, Loughborough

Boys And Girls

One day there were three girls in Year 5, they were called Sunita, Emma and Hailey. They were enemies with three boys called Scary Face, Rabbit's Teeth and Big Fat Ears. One Sunday Emma was walking in the forest because she wanted to see some pretty flowers. Rabbit had been hiding in the bush and he jumped out and hit her on the head with a book. Emma was crying and she felt very cross. She went home and told Sunita and Hailey. They decided to get back at the boy.

One day the boys were playing in a football match at school. The girls went to watch and got a fork and poked the football so through the match it started to go *sssssssss* and lose air. The girls started laughing and ran off, and the boys chased after them. The boys couldn't catch up and the girls ran home for dinner.

The next day the boys took Sunita's swimming costume from her bag and hung it at the boys' toilet window. Sunita screamed at the boys and got a teacher to tell them off and the boys got detention. The girls got into trouble too because they had been screaming. The teachers made them have detention too. Later that day they all stayed behind and did detention. Afterwards the girls and the boys made friends because they were all cross with the teachers. They went home and had sausages and chips for tea, and had a party.

Leah Wright (12)
Maplewell Hall Special School, Loughborough

Emily's Story

Once upon a time there were three children, they were called Emily, Luke and Daniel. They were taken on holiday by their parents and used to play on the beach.

One day they were playing football and Luke was kidnapped. He was taken by a big monster to a castle. He was kidnapped because the monster wanted to eat Luke's clothes.

The rest of the children got together and decided to rescue Luke. They decided that they would go to the castle and use a sword to rescue Luke, so they killed the monster and Luke was rescued.

The children went home and had curry for tea, to celebrate.

Emily Golding (16)
Maplewell Hall Special School, Loughborough

My Bad Dream

In 1939 the Second World War started, I was only 8 years old. Me and my mum went to the shop and got the newspaper. It said, 'Evacuate your children because a war has broken out'. A tear came out of my mum's eye.

Mum and me ran home, we listened to the radio. It said, 'Evacuate your children,' again and again. My dad came in, he said, 'I am going in the army.'

'No, no you can't,' said Mum.

My dad left. I went to bed, an air raid started. I suddenly woke up and panicked. I ran downstairs. I saw my mum dead on the floor. The Nazi soldiers had shot her. I shouted, 'Help, help!'

Then my dad came in, he said, 'Where's your mum?' He looked on the floor, he ran upstairs.

In the morning I shouted, 'Dad, Dad.' I went upstairs, I opened the door, I screamed for mercy. My dad had hung himself. I ran downstairs. I lived in Germany. I went to Australia then I went to Perth.
I set up a wounded soldiers' hospital. I got a telegram, it said, *'Your parents funeral is next week'*.

I went back to Germany. At the airport, a man said, 'Hi Sam, it's your dad.'

'No, no,' I suddenly fainted.

'Wake up, wake up, Sam.'

'Oh sorry. It was only a dream. I am never leaving you again! I love you Mum and Dad.'

Jakob Whiten (13)
Maplewell Hall Special School, Loughborough

My Day And Night At War

In the First World War there was a man called Tom Smith, he was a soldier for England. Tom fought in the trenches, he had a gun to shoot the enemy. Tom slept in the trenches.

One night he had a nightmare, he dreamt that he would die the next day. Tom woke up very afraid. Tom decided to write a letter to his mother and father in case it was his last day. During the day he got ready to fight, he got his gun together and all his kit. The men waited and waited and waited.

In the evening some people came and told the soldiers to go over the top and start fighting when they heard the whistle. Suddenly they heard the whistle. Tom got on all his kit and he climbed up the ditch and bombs were dropping from the sky. Tom ran across no-man's-land. It was bad here, it was muddy. There was a lot of water and dead people on the ground. Tom felt very sad and angry, and he got his gun out and shot the enemy. Then Tom ran back to the trenches where he lay. He had been shot in the leg, so Tom was sent back home to his mum and dad. They felt very happy to see him.

Jason Hadley (14)
Maplewell Hall Special School, Loughborough

The Kidnapped Horses

One day there was a girl called Megan and she lived in Australia, she loved horses. Megan went to work one morning and a boy came for a job. Joseph had blonde hair, blue eyes and he was very fit. Megan used to go to the gym too. Megan and Joseph started dating and they fell in love.

One day Joseph and Megan woke up at the same time. Megan looked out the window. 'Where are the horses?'

Then Joseph said, 'You are sad, you are having a joke!' They got dressed to go and look for the horses. Megan started to cry because she wanted her horses back. They got into the car to go and look for them. 'Which way do you think they have gone?' said Joseph.

'Let's try north,' said Megan. They saw an open gate and tyre marks. Mud was on the road. They followed the path as quickly as they could. Suddenly in the distance they could see a big, slow lorry.

They followed it for a long time until it pulled into a factory where they killed horses for meat. Megan screamed and shouted, 'Stop, stop the car we need to go and rescue the horses.' They saw them take out the horses. Joseph phoned the police but they were going to take half an hour and that would be too long. Joseph went up to the men and offered them money and got the horses back. The men got in the lorry and tried to escape with the money but Megan had let the lorry tyres down. The police arrived and arrested the men.

Megan and Joseph went home and Joseph asked Megan to marry him. They lived near the beach and had a baby. It was beautiful and they lived happily ever after.

Dannielle Thornton (12)
Maplewell Hall Special School, Loughborough

Which Witch Is Which?

'I accuseth you of being a witch!' These words buzzed around the town ever since the mayor hired a 'witch hunter'. The town was peaceful, friendly, the only strange things started to happen when the hunter arrived! Many of the townsfolk have been accused of witchcraft, whether it's sneezing or hiccuping. Others just can't see that behind that bushy beard there's a villain, one who wants to suck the town dry of money and 'witches'.

I rose early on Monday morn to witness the trial of the town's blacksmith. The hunter began, 'I accuseth you on two accounts of witchcraft!' Many gasps came from the crowd who gathered there.

'What are the accounts Mr Hunter?' enquired the mayor. The hunter carried on his trial.

'How doth ye plead?'

Silence.

'If ye not confess, in the stocks shall ye stay!' More gasps. It was now that I started noticing his tone of voice.

I shrieked, 'Mr Hunter I accuseth you of being a witch!' Everyone turned to look at me.

'On what accounts?' asked the hunter.

I continued, 'Ye feet doth not touch the ground!'

Maria Brown (13)
St Benedict's RC School, Derby

Colt Python

'Max, are you there?'

'Yeah.'

'Max let's get to the point, your new code name is Colt Python, remember this is a stealth mission if the New York terrorists see you they will shoot. Get in, get the PM and get out.'

'Sergeant, no weapons?'

'They were too heavy for the shuttle, you won't need them.'

Colt stood up and checked himself. He was wearing an indoor ops uniform. He checked the surroundings; there was an enemy up ahead. He stalked up behind him and wrenched his arm up his back. 'Where's the PM?' interrogated Colt.

'I ain't telling you … *argh!* The prison complex!' Colt knocked him out and headed for the main entrance.

Colt crept down the corridor and was at the prison complex. As he got to the cells he was seen on CCTV, immediately guards stormed the area. Colt woke up in the prison cell.

Colt finally persuaded the guard to give him the cigarettes, little did he know they were filled with anaesthetic gas and was blown into the guard's face. He fell to the ground; Colt took the keys and escaped. But the leader of the terrorists was waiting at the exit - Sniper Shark. A fight ensued with blows to the torso and head but finally Sniper Shark won, he looked at the cigarettes in the top pocket of Colt's shirt.

'Don't mind if I do!' laughed Sniper Shark and sucked in the cigarette. He fell; Colt rescued the PM. It was over.

Thomas Wilkinson (13)
St Benedict's RC School, Derby

Lee Thompson

During training, Lee was battered by the wind, harshly interrogated by top CIA forces, badly beaten for the information and called numerous profanities.

Now this was for real, Lee was hunting for a huge beast, loose in the Amazon forest. Armed with an upgraded M-16; it had laser sights and pure silver bullets which could kill any demon beast. Lee was wearing camouflage clothing; the design was tiger stripes which matched the surroundings. On his jacket, he had at least 4 grenades hanging from his middle pocket and a belt which ran across his body, lined with another 50 bullets.

Lee dropped to prone as he spotted the huge brown beast. It was munching on the remains of which looked like some other human who had tried to slaughter the beast. Lee got up and walked towards the monster. 'Oi, you, I'll take you down!' The monster carried on chewing at the bony carcass. Lee then pulled out his M-16 and shot it in the back. 'Now that I have your attention!' The beast growled and started galloping at him, he pulled up his gun and shot it furiously at the monster - it slumped to the ground, it hit the ground with a thump and its head rolled away - he had beheaded the beast.

Proudly he walked away but something didn't feel right. He looked down and saw a 15-inch claw embedded in his chest, he felt pain and also slumped to the ground to join the beast.

Adam Fraczek (13)
St Benedict's RC School, Derby

The Terrible Toy

'Just shut up!' I shouted at my brother. 'Stop annoying me!' I was on my way to the toy shop.

'Don't shout,' my brother said. Then I saw it. The latest toy called Captain Crusher. I ran inside to buy it. I then rushed home and as I opened the door, 'It's nearly 9.00, go to bed,' Mum said. Despite my objections, I had to go to bed.

I was asleep for a while when, suddenly, I was awoken by a strange noise. I sat up in bed and saw a figure standing on the bed. It was pointing something at me and started walking towards me. *'Argh! it's alive!'* I exclaimed.

'Stop shouting,' ordered my brother. 'What is it?'

'That toy tried to kill me,' I said. The toy was lying lifelessly on the bed.

'Don't be stupid,' he replied, walking out of the room. The toy stood up holding a toy gun and a real knife. I jumped out of bed and ran to the opposite side of my room.

'You will be eliminated!' it proclaimed. The gun was fired, the bullet smashed into my wall just missing my head. It wasn't a toy! It jumped off the bed and stood by the door.

I was trapped. It lifted the gun up and pointed it at me. I was terrified. It fell to the ground lifelessly. My brother came in laughing at me.

'Don't worry, it's radio controlled,' he said, holding a controller.

Ben Bullivant (13)
St Benedict's RC School, Derby

Roger's Revenge

I always wondered what it would be like to be a hamster and now I know ...

It was just an ordinary day, I walked to school and met Francis, the school bully, who took my dinner money and I entered the school gates and went to my corner. Suddenly I spotted a small tanned boy. He had black hair which covered one of his big brown eyes and long dark eyelashes. His stunningly white teeth gleamed.

'What do you want?' I snapped.

'I have come to give you something.' Out of his pocket he produced a small round pendant on a thin gold chain. On one side it had a picture of a wolf jumping through a ring of flames.

'What is it for?' I asked, but he was already gone.

I put it on and went to my classroom where Francis pushed me over and the pendant fell from my neck. I grabbed it and said to myself, 'I wish I could get my own back on Francis!'

With a puff of green smoke I turned into Roger, Class 4D's hamster, this was Francis' class. *This is my chance,* I thought. I could see him sitting right in front of the cage, I opened the door and climbed out, I went down the table leg and onto his shoulder. Then I jumped and attached myself onto his nose. Blood was everywhere.

Francis was off school for ages and no one knows why Roger attacked him like that.

Natalie Barratt (13)
St Benedict's RC School, Derby

Twinkle-Toes Job!

Ring, ring! Twinkle-Toes woke up. It was her alarm. Another tooth had fallen out of a precious child. Out of her magical princess house she came. She fluttered out onto the white, fluffy, sparkling clouds. Through the sky she flew until she reached 18 Magical Lane. Cindy-Loo was fast asleep. Her first tooth had fallen out.

Twinkle lay on the bed, took the baby tooth, cleaned it and put it into her diamond, pink gemmed box. She then reached out of her pocket some fairy dust and sprinkled it over Cindy. She then took out of her pocket a pound coin and placed it under the pillow. She flickered back to her home and laid in her bed, small as a pea!

The following morning Cindy woke up, so anxious, she fell off her bed. 'Daddy, Daddy, I've got a pound!' She was filled with happiness, delight and joy. Twinkle looked over, with a wink of an eye and a huge grin.

Katie McCabe (12)
St Benedict's RC School, Derby

A Day In The Life Of A Tree!

It all happened so suddenly! I didn't believe something so magical would happen to me. Now I am 21 I can tell my story. Banga Busher told me to wait 10 years till I spoke out and now I have.

I was walking home back from school. I walked through the same woods and paths. There in front of me I saw it, a deer, it had been caught in a trap. I knelt down next to it, I stroked it and it sharply moved and bellowed loudly, it echoed through the woods. I quietly crept behind, full of fear, and undid the trap.

Suddenly a gush of wind knocked me off my feet and pushed me to the floor again. There before me stood a dark man with black spiky hair. The only clothing he had on was a wrap around his waist to his knees.

'Elsa,' he said. 'You have broken the spell of Banga Busher, now you may have one wish, but wish carefully child.'

My wish was to be a tree, I don't know why but it was. I said to Banga, 'Just for one day I would like to be a tree!'

Suddenly I was a tree. The strange-looking man had vanished. Then I felt something, the leaves on me whooshed in the wind. I felt like I was on cloud nine.

Ohh ahh, what is happening, my head's bursting. Where am I? I never understood why I ended up on this hilltop and how.

Olivia McCalla (12)
St Benedict's RC School, Derby

The Banshee

In Ireland lived a girl who cried at night as she sat on a hill alone. Her name was the banshee, nobody had seen her, until a little girl got lost.

She saw the banshee and said, 'I thought it was a girl but when I saw her, her body was covered in hair. She just sat there, her long black hair on her head. I couldn't believe my eyes!' The girl told me, as if the banshee were in the room.

The girl's name was Maureen. The reason why she was so shocked was because the banshee was only an Irish myth and legend. The girl never went back there even as she grew older, but she still hears the banshee's cry echo through the hills at night. The girl tells stories of the banshee now, but till this day the banshee has not been seen again.

Grace Greene-Gallagher (12)
St Benedict's RC School, Derby

A Day In The Life Of A Bird

One day there was a girl called Shelby. She was 10 years old and had an evil stepmother, who looked after her. Every time Shelby got sent up to her room she would look out of her window and she wished that she would transform into a beautiful white bird.

The next day Shelby was in massive trouble and, as usual, got sent up to her room, but this time it was different. The evil stepmother got so mad that she turned Shelby into a beautiful golden bird. Shelby looked into her mirror and was amazed at what she saw. She got up on the window ledge and looked out to the hills and valleys beyond, she took a deep breath of air and stretched her wings out and dropped herself out of the window, and then to her amazement she was flying on top of the trees.

By this time it was getting dark and Shelby was getting scared. Then she heard a squawking coming her way then everything went dead ...

Maeve Nethercott (12)
St Benedict's RC School, Derby

Gorgon's Hollow

Harold looked at the sign outside the cave, *Gorgon's Hollow* it proclaimed. Harold thought back to his schooldays, remembering Medusa, the snake-haired gorgon whose terrible stare turned men to stone. He sat down and waited for his parents to come back out. He had sat for 30 minutes when he began to wonder where they'd got to.

'Mum? Dad?' he shouted. There was no answer. Harold sat for another ten minutes before he decided to investigate. He stepped into the darkness and a sudden chill overcame him. Harold stepped in further. He got about 20 metres into the cave when a sudden light came from behind him. Harold looked around and saw hundreds of stone statues. They almost looked real, but every one of them was looking over their shoulders. Images of Medusa flared in his mind's eye. A strange shadow was cast next to his - a woman with writhing hair. Harold looked over his shoulder …

James Varney (12)
St Benedict's RC School, Derby

Gorgon's Journey

In a queer place in the middle of nowhere there were tribes. These tribes were different goblin families. In the Asqad tribe there was a middle-aged goblin called Sargan. He was strong and his father was the leader of the tribe. He was the youngest in the family and he had nine older brothers. Most of the time he got left out and rejected. He hated his life.

One nog (the goblin word for day), his father turned drastically ill. He had a disease which couldn't be cured using goblin remedies. There was only one cure for it which was gorn, the gorns lived miles and miles away and they hated goblins.

That night Gorgon and his brothers had a serious meeting. They knew that if their father died they'd never decide who got to be the leader so they had to cure him. 'I will go,' said Sargan. He thought that if he saved his father he would be respected so he packed and off he went.

Ted Kemplen (12)
St Benedict's RC School, Derby

The Manager

Adam, the manager of Nokia, slumped back in his chair. It had been a long day and one he would remember for a long time. Staring out at the rocket he thought long and hard, searching for an answer to his problems. What did he know? John and Paul had skipped the country taking all the profits from his Mars project and leaving him with all the debt.

Then an idea entered his head. If he could hack into some big bank then he could get away with no proof of who stole it. This would be an impossible task for the average computer nerd but he was no ordinary geek. It was also a great opportunity to show off his new computer to all his colleagues. Of course he would never really do this but these where exceptional circumstances.

John Perry and Paul Spiller were just landing in Heathrow. England was a lovely spot to settle down with a few billion. John handed the accountant his card and watched Paul fumble for his comb only to have his card back in two halves. The accountant at the desk had cut it.

They returned home a day later in a prison van moneyless and facing several charges of theft and one for hitching a ride with no money.

Adam cracked a knuckle. It was funny how two wrongs could sometimes make a right.

Mark Roe (13)
St Benedict's RC School, Derby

Egor And The Dragon

In the deepest depths of Camelot, lived a wizard named Magnus. Magnus had an extremely long beard just below his feet and he always tripped over it. Magnus also had a rather ugly helper. Named Egor he hardly had any hair, he wore rags and was a disgusting green.

One day Magnus decided to buy a dragon from the market.

'Egor, Egor, come here!' yelled Magnus.

'Yes Master,' replied Egor in a croaky voice.

'I want you to fetch me a dragon from the market,' said Magnus.

Egor was shocked but he put on his cloak and put up his hood and set out to the market.

There Egor found a man in a little snicket way.

'Excuse me, do you know where I can find a ... dragon?' whispered Egor.

'Here's one,' replied the sick old man. The man clicked his fingers and an evil red-eyed dragon appeared. Egor looked amazed, the dragon frowned at him.

'Nice dragon, nice dragon,' stuttered Egor.

The dragon opened his mouth and swallowed Egor in one.

'Good dragon,' said the sick old man, 'you can go home now,' and the man clicked his fingers and the dragon disappeared.

Eventually the old wizard died of boredom waiting for Egor to return with his dragon and the sick old man carried on letting his dragon eat people.

Ashleigh Warman-Dawes (12)
St Benedict's RC School, Derby

The Day In The Life Of A Kitten

'What's that?' exclaimed Shadow climbing over a brick wall. Down below there was overgrown garden. The thing Shadow had been interested in was just a flowerpot. She investigated it, happily seeing if she could fit inside.

'What are your doing Shortie?' said a gruff voice. 'This is my area.'

There was a big black cat standing over the flowerpot.

'I was just playing in this flowerpot,' said Shadow timidly.

'That flowerpot's mine, too,' the cat said. 'Could you leave please?'

'No,' said Shadow, getting bolder, 'I want to play here.'

The big cat chased Shadow over the wall. Shadow ran so fast she tripped and hurt her paw. The big cat left her and went back. Her owner found her.

'Oh no, look at Shadow's paw,' her owner said. 'Better take her to the vet.'

The vet, isn't that a place where they stick needles in you? Shadow thought.

'No,' she shouted, 'I don't want to go.'

But all her owner heard was 'miaow'.

Heather Cripps (11)
St Benedict's RC School, Derby

The Boy Who Cried Bye

There was once a little boy named John who lived in a house with his mum. He had no friends or anybody to play with until today. He found out he was moving to a neighbourhood with loads of people of his own age.

After the move they settled in very well and John made friends.

On one stormy night John and his friends went out down into the woods. They were at their new base where they hung out together. Then all of a sudden lightning struck their base and it fell to the floor. Whilst trying to get out they had to walk under a lot of trees.

10 minutes later another lightning strike hit one of John's friends. As they carried on walking they heard a howl and crunching noises like somebody was following them but nobody was there.

All of a sudden John and his friends were trapped. They turned around and …

Matthew Regan (12)
St Benedict's RC School, Derby

A Day In The Life Of A Forgotten Teddy

'Er ... hello,' Patch had said timidly, venturing towards a posh, fluffy pink teddy, sat on his place of the bed. That was where it all began, he sighed, shrinking deeper into his cardboard box. He sat for a while thinking, before he was startled by a loud rumble.

'Oh, it's just my tummy,' he mumbled to himself, getting up to search in old bean cans. Unluckily, some others were looking for their tea too.

'Grr!' Patch jumped and looked behind him and the dogs began the chase.

'Stop! Go away!' screamed Patch as the dogs caught up, drool streaming from their mouths like waterfalls.

Patch tripped on a can and the dogs dived on top of him, luckily he found a steak in a can.

'H-hey boys,' Patch stammered, holding up the steak, 'how about a juicy steak instead of a bag of fluff?'

Obviously they went for the steak. As Patch chucked it they ran after it clumsily. As Patch turned to run he noticed an odd pain in his arm. He looked down, blood oozed out. After all he'd been through he couldn't stand anymore and fainted.

When he finally awoke and opened his eyes he saw a grubby but kind face peering down at him.

'Oh you poor thing,' cried the girl picking him up and running back to her damp campfire where she bandaged Patch up and nursed him back to health.

Anna Cripps (13)
St Benedict's RC School, Derby

Last Again

'I pick ... Nile,' Jordan said, whilst picking teams for football on the playground. Everyone was picked but Tom, he hated being picked last, it happened every day at lunchtime and he was always embarrassed as he caused a fight with the team captains.

'Have him on your team,' they all said in rage and it wasted half their football time. He ended up going on Sean's team (Jordan's opponent), he had to play as far away from the ball as possible they all said laughing their heads off.

The game started. The pitch was very soggy and immediately somehow the ball rolled to Tom. Everyone chased him and Jordan went flying straight into him and knocked him unconscious. Everyone thought that was humorous except Tom, who laid on the floor trying not to cry.

'I wish I could be great at football, no one would laugh at me and maybe I would be picked first.' All of a sudden a puff of smoke appeared over Tom. A man appeared with a black suit. He then started speaking a different language, then disappeared. Tom got up and all of a sudden he started playing wonderfully and scoring many goals, but then he got more excited as he was picked first. The next game a new boy came to school and got laughed at, he felt guilty. Be careful what you wish for.

Christopher Ruston (12)
St Benedict's RC School, Derby

Charlie Caterpillar

There is a caterpillar named Charlie, he is a light green colour and lives in a greenhouse in somebody's garden. He wakes up in the morning and has a shower when the owners of the greenhouse water their plants. Then he nibbles at a few leaves for breakfast and goes out to play with his friends; Billy Butterfly, Sammy Spider, Lucy Ladybird, Annie Ant, Molly Moth, Bobby Bee and Wally Wasp.

Today he and his friends decided to have a picnic. They were going to give Lucy Ladybird a surprise birthday party, so Billy got everyone together and told them about it. Sammy made spiderweb decorations, Annie kept Lucy busy, Molly gathered food, Bobby and Wally got some honey for her cake and Charlie got a leaf from a plant and sat it next to a big rock in the shade so they wouldn't get too hot.

When they had finished Annie brought Lucy over to the party and all of the others ran to hide. Lucy closed her eyes and when she opened them the others jumped out and shouted, 'Surprise!'

'Oh wow, thank you so much,' Lucy said and then everyone sat down to eat.'

'This cake is great,' said Charlie.

Everyone agreed with him. After the food Lucy opened her presents, she thanked everybody. Then they danced and joked and played party games for ages, even when it got dark because Freddy Firefly came over with his friends to give some light over the party. Everyone said goodnight and went to bed. Charlie climbed into his leaf and soil bed and said, 'Hmm, what an exciting day, I wonder what I'll do tomorrow?' Then he fell fast asleep.

Jessica Kate Coupland (12)
St Benedict's RC School, Derby

Life Is Precious, Life Is Sweet

'But Mum!' I yelled. 'All my mates are going. They have already bought a ticket for me!'

'No you are not going to a rock concert, it will leave permanent damage to your ears!' Mum answered calmly.

'It's not fair!' I screamed. I stormed out of the kitchen. The concert was in twenty minutes. I shoved my pillow under my bed covers, got dressed and made-up and snuck out of the window. Mum is so thick, she'd never guess.

I met Grace, Heather and Jess at the concert hall. We all went in chatting excitedly.

The concert was great! When we came out it was pitch-black. As I only lived up the road, I walked back to my house. As I was crossing the road a car swerved round the corner. I stood there frozen. The car hit me. I just laid in the middle of the road. No one was around. The car drove off. I remembered a poem I knew when I was little.

'Life is precious, life is sweet,
But Heaven's door is what I now meet.
I should have lived a better life
Not concentrated on trouble and strife,
But now it's all over for me
Try and live your own life with glee'.

Then I saw a bright light and my soul floated towards it. A tear trickled down my ghostly face. 'Sorry Mum,' I whispered. 'I love you really!'

Aisling Lammond (12)
St Benedict's RC School, Derby

A Day In The Life Of Marty The Cat

Marty was a stray cat. Every day he would wander around the streets looking for food. But at night Marty became a different cat. He and his friends were the hardmen of the cat world. They smoked in people's faces and started fights with the other cat gangs. Tonight was no different …

'What did you just say to me?' Marty stared at his enemy with his sinister yellow eyes.

I said, 'You're so dumb you got ran over by a parked car!'

Marty was now fuming with anger. 'Are you starting a fight?' said Marty.

'Bring it on?' replied the cat. The fight broke out.

It wasn't long before other cats joined in. The fight in the park lasted for ages. It soon moved out of the park and onto the streets. Running after the biggest cat it scratched him on the stomach, Marty found himself in the middle of the road. A truck drove straight at him. It went straight over Marty and left him without a scratch. There was a word on the back. *Stop!* It was a sign.

'Join the fight, Marty we need you,' said his friend. Marty didn't say a word. He wandered off into the moonlight. The hardman cat had seen the error of his ways.

Tom Hall (12)
St Benedict's RC School, Derby

The Lost Village Of Hallsands

It was January 1917 and I sat on the harbour waiting for Edward to come back from fishing. The smell of fish and seaweed drifted around the village, the streets were packed with lobster pots and fishing nets, smoke billowed from the chimneys and the salty seawater lapped up near my feet.

Fishermen grunted and groaned, hauling crates of fish from their boats, I overheard them saying there would be a big storm that night.

I looked out, remembering the gravel bank. When I was young I had watched the men take the gravel from the bank and it dropped 20 feet below sea level and now out of view, my thoughts were interrupted by someone calling my name. 'Elisa, Elisa.' I turned round to see Eddy, then stood up and ran to him, relieved that he was safe as a storm was brewing.

The storm continued to build up in the next three hours and during supper. Mr Biggs came round and told us to move to high ground. "Tis gonna be a big 'un,' he said.

We grabbed some bags and packed them. Then me and my family joined the other villagers walking up the road. Screaming from behind made us turn back: a huge wave crashed into a house knocking it to the sea and people with it, we could do nothing but watch and cry and clamber up into the hills.

We never returned home. The sea claimed everything we owned.

Lucy Windall (12)
St Mary's RC High School, Hereford

A Day In The Life Of A Rocker

'Urrgh!' I moaned furiously as my alarm went off! After about ten minutes my little annoying sister, Stephanie, came up and pinched me! I hate her; I jumped out of bed and threw her out my door. (Practically!) Mum was calling me to hurry up, but I was ready to go in a second!

Saints and Devils came round after school (that's our band). We were halfway through a song called 'Midnight Shock' when my mobile went off! I had great news! My mate knows this guy from the greatest and biggest concert house and they needed another band to perform.

The next day we went into the middle of the town to audition. We were brilliant and the fat, grumpy man let us in!

We practised whenever we could for that final week. It sounded amazing and so wicked it could blow the head off anyone! Our band was so excited! I couldn't believe it! Our first *ever* concert, I couldn't wait!

The day had finally come, it was here! I got up at 6am that morning, I got dressed and I checked everything twice or more over so that I didn't forget anything!

At 10 o'clock I got in the car and my mum dropped me off. It was fab! We had 15 minutes to go, so I got set up! I thought it was going to be brilliant, but it didn't turn out that way …

Lucie Rivers (11)
St Mary's RC High School, Hereford

A Day In The Life Of My Very Lazy Cat Ibby

I woke up, went back to sleep.

I woke up looked for some food, there wasn't any so I went back to sleep.

I woke up, there was some food and a lot of tall humans walking around. I had breakfast, walked upstairs to find a comfortable bed and fell asleep again.

I was rudely awoken by some smaller, annoying human bouncing on the bed, they have no respect for my needs. They soon left so I relaxed back into the covers and fell asleep yet again. It was a very quiet day so I slept for five hours.

I woke up again and ate some more food. I walked to the door and waited for someone to open the door. Surprisingly it was warm outside and not as cold as it usually is. I walked down the steps to the bottom of the garden and climbed over the fence and into the long grass on the other side, which needed cutting. Then I walked down the slope and onto the path that goes all the way from one end of the street to the other. I looked for some shade under the trees and fell asleep.

Something brushed past me, a dark shadow. It was dark already! I must have slept for ages. I walked back up the slope, over the fence, raced up the steps and through the open door and walked slowly to my basket and ... fell asleep.

Natasha MacMahon (12)
St Mary's RC High School, Hereford

The Alien Hunt

The starship 'Thunder-Zap' had been flying through space for about 15 years searching for extraterrestrial lifeforms. So far they haven't found anything.

The Thunder-Zap was travelling in the Dog's Leg Nebula at speeds of over 1,000,000mph. This was quite slow for a ship but it was driving slowly on purpose because it had just picked up a strange signal.

'Have you still got a signal, Lt?' asked Captain Johnson.

'Yes Sir, it's getting stronger,' replied Lt Doyle, 'but what's strange is that we have never had a signal before and now we're getting a really strong one, do you think it could be an ambush?'

'Absolutely not!' snapped the captain. 'Now keep an eye on that signal!'

Lt Doyle returned to his screen, very annoyed.

Suddenly the signal cut off and there was total silence.

A flash of bright light came from a window. Everyone crowded around the window and stared in amazement as a huge UFO slowly moved past them. A small door on the UFO started to open and loads of little spaceships shot out; they started shooting at the Thunder-Zap!

'Quick!' shouted the captain. 'To your stations!'

Everyone ran, they got to their places and the ship zoomed away, Lt Doyle looked back and was horrified because all the little ships were chasing them.

'Captain,' he cried, 'look!'

The captain looked back and his jaw dropped. 'Activate the shield and guns!'

Brrrving, bang, bang!' The Thunder-Zap was doing her best, but it wasn't good enough.

Boom! ...

Dominic Wylor-Owen (14)
St Mary's RC High School, Hereford

The Outlaw's Revenge

It was a very hot day in Ghost City and Johnny Ynnhoj was visiting his granny. As he drove along the dusty road, dust clouds were blowing in his face. Johnny was carrying a case that was full of money and he held this very tightly. As the truck drove faster the dust clouds got thicker until it was too much, he put the case down to say something but was careful because he had heard about the most feared outlaw in the southern states, Lucy Crag, known as Lonely Lucy Crag. He asked the driver if he could close his window, checking the case every second.

The car came to a stop and Johnny turned to the driver, what Johnny then found out was that the driver was actually French and couldn't understand a word he was saying. Johnny spent a lot of time talking to him and when he looked back, the case was gone!

Johnny ran out of the car and saw a tall, good-looking lady wearing a cowboy hat and a sheriff's badge. Johnny had just fallen into the trap of Lonely Lucy Crag.

Johnny starred into the eyes of the outlaw and said, 'That's mine.'

The driver looked out of the window and at the first sight of Lucy he sped off. It was only Johnny, Lucy and the desert, but what Johnny didn't know was who was going to survive.

This was the last we saw of Johnny and Lonely Lucy Crag.

James Pember (13)
St Mary's RC High School, Hereford

The Sighting

The sky was black, the thunder was crashing down on the little wooden shack in the mountains of Austria.

Jim Wooden lived in this humble hut. When he was younger Jim swore to his mum he saw UFOs at night around that shack. Maybe this was an alien activity area. It is never sunny and there's never good weather in these mountains, it is constantly raining.

That night, Friday 13th 1991, Jim saw the sightings again, exactly 60 years after seeing them when he was a child. When he made eye contact with this shining silver ship in the thick clouds there was an enormous crash of thunder shaking Jim's shack. The ship shot across the sky trying to stay out of sight but Jim was mesmerised by this ship. He tried to forget what he'd seen when he was out of the trance, but it shot past again making him focus on what it was doing out here.

He went back inside his shack, the thunder still crashing down. He heard the ship shooting past another four times. He thought maybe because he saw it, it was now looking for him but he got in the shack when the ship was in the thick black clouds.

After a day of hiding from the mysterious ship it must have given up and must have gone back to its home planet.

Now every Friday 13th every 60 years this same ship comes back to that same shack in the mountains of Austria.

Alex Caine (14)
St Mary's RC High School, Hereford

A Day In The Life Of Ryan Giggs
(In the FA Cup Final against Arsenal)

Saturday 21st

I can't believe it, we were so close. We were the better side all game. I was disappointed that I didn't start; I came on in extra time. Ronaldo was amazing, I don't know where he got the energy from. Wayne Rooney had some great chances, Arsenal had about 3 chances if that. Arsenal didn't do anything all game. It went into penalties and we had one saved, that's how Arsenal won. We had Roy Carroll in goal. All the lads were well disappointed but there is always next season.

We have to keep our heads up and next season who knows what we can win. We didn't do that well this year but we can make up for it next time. Arsenal had one man sent off but right at the end of extra time so it didn't really make a difference. I don't believe that if you wear red you win, I mean just look at Chelsea they won the Premiership and their kit is blue. When I walked off that pitch I felt so upset and annoyed that we had been the better side and we'd still lost. Arsenal looked lost without their main striker Henry, well that's my opinion. Next time we meet Arsenal we will definitely beat them, I will make sure of that.

Natasha James (12)
St Mary's RC High School, Hereford

A Day In The Life Of Lucy Grimshaw

Lucy couldn't wait to go on holiday, though when Lucy began to pack, she had a weird feeling she'd never had before.

Later Lucy was tucked up in bed and ready to set sail the following morning.

The waves were rough. Lucy was on the boat. Then a flash of lightning shot across the sky, so she decided to go back to her cabin.

Just as Lucy had settled, she heard screaming. *Who's that?* she thought, as others continued screaming.

Lucy went onto the deck in her nightdress. She saw people crying. Then, she saw a horrific sight. A man had got onto the rail around the ship and jumped into the ocean. She screamed and looked over the side. He was gone.

'What's going on?' she asked a lady.

'The boat is sinking and there's no one to help,' she said.

Her heart sank.

Suddenly, Lucy awoke. 'Mum?' she said, as they had breakfast. 'Don't take the family on holiday, I had a dream that the ship sunk and everyone on the ship died!'

'I bet it was just one of your silly nightmares!' her mum said, chuckling.

'But what if it comes true, what if I'm right and the whole family dies?'

Lucy's mum cancelled the holiday. Two days later the family were watching the news. They announced a boat had been found, deserted in the middle of the ocean. It was called 'Midnight Cruiser'. She looked at her mum in amazement. That was their boat. Their death trap.

Stacey Hirst (11)
St Mary's RC High School, Hereford

A Day In The Life Of Jack Reynolds

January 17th 1915, France

Dear Vera,

Today we had a big drill, so that we could practice when the Germans come to fight. It was quite difficult, though I preferred it to the real thing. I miss you and the children dreadfully. Here is a poem I wrote for you:

Today was terrible,
   … yours was great.
   You have a warm house,
   … I have a trench.
   You have a bed with a warm fluffy pillow,
   … I have a rough sleeping bag with mud underneath.
   You see our children grow up and play,
   … while I see men dying and coughing to death.

Am I guilty, or am I a hero?
   Is this war worth it or is it pointless?
   Who will it help?
      England?
         The world?
            Or no one at all?
   I am so confused.
   Please write to me my love and kiss the children for me.

Lots of love, your dearest husband,
   Jack XXX.

Maysie Williams (12)
St Mary's RC High School, Hereford

A Day In The Life Of Homer Simpson

I woke up and ... fell asleep again. Work was boring as usual, but I found a fun new way of wearing my underpants over my head. Marge cooked steak and this weird thing that looked like a green tree. I wasn't sure what it was so I gave it to the dog. Marge served me a fine vintage of Duff. Next thing you know I had drunk a whole crate of them. Hey but that's what marriage is all about.

Bart was annoying me saying something about a fire at Ned Flanders' house but Flanders didn't invite me to his barbecue so I didn't help him. I sent out Maggie with a small bucket of petrol.

Call this number if you want to know how to wear your underpants over your head: 01568 924.

Joseph Langley (11)
St Mary's RC High School, Hereford

A Day In The Life Of Wayne Rooney

It was half-time and we were 11-0 down to Blackburn. Alex was yelling at me for getting 5 players sent off because I went around punching the other players and blaming it on Roy Keane but at the end of the day the loyal fans were behind me all the way, chanting, 'Ogre!' and 'with that face it brings down the word cosmetic surgery 6 feet under'.

Well I had my wonderful girlfriend on my side shouting, 'Hi honey!' Waving her 10 bags of designer clothes at me!

Finally the whistle for the end of the game.

Daniel Tanner (12)
St Mary's RC High School, Hereford

A Day In The Life Of My Dad's Car

'Night Mum,' I yawned to Mum.

'Goodnight ... see you in the morning,' Mum replied, seeming more engrossed in 'EastEnders' than me.

Today was OK, tomorrow will be better though. I thought of all the wonderful things I would be doing tomorrow as I drifted off to sleep.

The next morning I woke up with a shock, I could feel that this wasn't my body, it was like a metal and rusty feeling. I opened my eyes, I was on the drive!

I don't know how, I seemed to be my dad's car! Yes ... I was definitely that old, red, leather seated car!

This wasn't possible, I had just gone to bed and fallen asleep and then I was here. I thought, *oh no, here comes Dad*. I'd forgotten Dad was working away today. He sat down.

'Ouch,' I squeaked. It felt like giving him a piggyback.

He started the engine - heck it felt like a million people were pinching me. He started driving out of the street, it felt like I was using jet-powered Rollerblades!

We were now miles away from home, it was all fields. We were now miles further than that too. I could see in the distance a truck ... Dad hated these. 'Always taking up the road', he used to say. Dad didn't seem to slow down.

'Dad slow down,' I said. I seemed like he couldn't hear me. 'Dad slow down,' I now shouted. 'Dad you're going to *crash!*' I yelled.

Daniel Winter (12)
St Mary's RC High School, Hereford

A Day In The Life Of My Pet Cat

'Miaow, ahh. Well that was a nice nap, I think it's time for something to eat! Let's see. Wait a minute there's no one at home.'

The fat ginger cat strolled around the house, but he didn't find anyone, so he gave up and spread himself across the cream carpet.

'Oh look, someone's coming up the drive but it's not my fabulous family so who is it?'

It was a housekeeper, she walked into the house, sat on the sofa and went to sleep making herself at home.

'Hang on, I'm not having this, I'm just going to make noise until she wakes up!' The cat did this until the lady got up and fed him.

He didn't like this lady so Tigger had a plan to make the housekeeper's time a misery.

In five days Tigger had clawed the sofa, attempted to attack the lady and when she let the cat go outside he would bring in a dead mouse and hide it between the laundry and, last but not least, he would make as much noise as he possibly could at 11pm at night!

Tigger was furious when he found out that his owners had gone on holiday to Spain without him for two weeks, meanwhile Tigger was stuck with this housekeeper. Tigger made sure he would get his own back!

Kate Probert-Jones (12)
St Mary's RC High School, Hereford

A Day In The Life Of My Goldfish

'Ahh, morning mum! Morning Dad!' I opened my eyes and stretched. 'Ahh, I'm a goldfish! Oh this is new.' I was an orange, fat, slow fish and I had a three second memory span.

I think it started when that weird man asked me what my worst animal was, I said, 'Goldfish', then he held my head and chanted something funny.

'Oh would you look at that! What was I saying? Oh what a nice pebble we have here!' I kept starting off what seemed, my life again after every three seconds. I had a moment of cleverness, (if that's a word), to keep hitting the fish bowl till it fell to the ground then I wrote a note to myself quickly with pebbles.

I hit the glass for about three seconds, stopped, then swam around for a bit, saw the note and began to hit the glass again. This cycle continued for about five minutes until the whole bowl fell to the ground.

'Argh!' I screamed as I fell. Suddenly, before I could blink, my cat, yes, my cat! swooped off of the table and gobbled me up.

Now I'm in Tuftey's, my cat's digestive system. There was a small pool of fluid among all the other grime. To help me breathe I shuffled along to the pool and nestled my head in it. All of a sudden I felt a strange sensation in my fin and out from it grew a finger.

'Oh this is new,' I added, than *bang!* The cat exploded and I was stood in the middle of the dining room.

'Oh hello darling. Um, where's the cat?' Mum asked, looking around for the cat.

'I ... um ... I don't know,' I stuttered.

I had definitely had enough of being a ... *goldfish!*

Bronwyn Townsend (12)
St Mary's RC High School, Hereford

A Day In The Life Of Marilyn Monroe

The sun rose over California beaming into the laced bedroom of Marilyn. With her two marriages over life was hard on her own. Marilyn wrenched herself out of bed and sighed. She had to start filming in an hour.

Life is hard at 36. All of a sudden you feel old and unwanted in the world. Your star potential goes downhill and being alone never helps. Today is August 4th and there are 27 days left of filming. I have been counting. I feel so low but why, Norma, why? Norma, no one has called me by my real name for years. I think Norma Jean is such a pretty name, all the more reason for me to go start a new life somewhere where I can't come back and I shall be called Norma Jean as I once was. I shall leave California for good, I'll just press the buttons on my phone pad and call the film company and tell them I can't make it today.

There, I'm not going in to work today. I'm taking a day to plan what I shall do tonight. I'll leave my things as they are but I'll take a trip to a chemist and get some more painkillers for my head or maybe I'll lock myself in my room and just fall asleep, just doze off. This is most likely the last time I'll write to you, I won't take you with me.

Amalie Millest (13)
St Mary's RC High School, Hereford

A Day In The Life Of A Desert Girl

A whistling wind winds its way around my dress. Dunes spread before me, rising and falling like my breath. I survey my land. My kingdom. Here in the desert I am free. The sky's compassionate eye stares upon my starlit journey, mirroring the loneliness. Alone I travel, graceful and accustomed to the sands I glide like a rattlesnake. I am on this journey for a reason. A light wind billows my dress, sand grains tickle my feet. Only here is the world at peace, just me, the sky and the sands. Stars twinkle with the intensity of diamonds, flickering candles of hope under the oppression of a black, velvet curtain. My hair tickles the back of my neck, my nose stud shimmers like a star. My kingdom can be altered with a breath of wind, flowing like water it changes forever, with me riding upon the waves. I flow over the sand like a bird over clouds. This is where I belong. I am hunting for water, to keep my family alive.

Holding my head high, I walk elegantly, balancing my pots on my head. Out of the dusty dunes something twinkles, shimmering like the gracing stars. A cool calmness surrounds me as I approach the oasis. Water seems solid, but the slightest ripple breaks it, a mirror, a gem, a magical drop from a star. Here in the desert, all is silent as I stand beside the water. I am alone. Just me, the sky and the sands.

Emily Lunn (12)
St Mary's RC High School, Hereford

Gunshot

The warm, delicious smell of fish and chips was slowly wafting up the line to where I was standing. I took a deep sniff and breathed in the smell, much to the disgust of the rather pompous man standing in front.

The queue in the shop shifted a few steps forward and I looked up at the tempting menu. I decided on fish and chips. Rattling my change, I looked out of the glass front of the shop. Several youths were gathering outside, chattering nineteen to the dozen. They looked quite menacing with their hoodies up.

'Yes?' a woman behind the counter asked me.

'Um, 1 fish and chips, please,' I ordered and placed my money on the warm counter.

'£2.50, please,' said the woman and collected my change off the counter. She placed it in the till and began to sort out my order. A few minutes later, a package was shoved into my hands and I was barged out of the line.

As I walked out of the shop, I began to open the package. Suddenly there was a deafening *bang*, unmistakingly, a gunshot. A young man about ten feet from me sank to his knees and the group of youths ran off, looking terrified. I ran to the bleeding man. People were walking up, looking concerned. I turned and faced the people.

'Cop! Detective Constable Smith, CID,' I shouted. 'Stay back!' I pulled out my mobile phone, sighing - this was supposed to be my night off!

Kathryn Martin (13)
St Mary's RC High School, Hereford

A Day In The Life Of Isabella Silvas

The Titanic, the world's largest liner they said. Everybody wanted to go on it, but I was the lucky one. Dad said I should be grateful and thank God for my good fortune and to pray for a safe journey. But everyone said I didn't need to, 'God himself could not sink the Titanic,' that's what they said.

I woke up, it was a normal day aboard the great ship and we were getting closer and closer to America. I decided to look around the ship so I went off on my own to look around. I decided to go to the ballroom; it was so beautiful, with huge chandeliers and an orchestra playing in the corner. I danced around pretending to wear a lovely ballgown and be dancing with a rich young man from America, who desperately wanted my hand in marriage.

The rest of the day was spent exploring and before I knew it, it was time for a sumptuous dinner before falling into bed. I was just drifting off to sleep when I heard a loud shriek from upstairs; my parents were fast asleep so I decided to go and see for myself. I went up to deck, there was ice everywhere on deck. The ship had collided with a huge iceberg.

As people rushed for safety, screaming and shouting I felt my dad grab my hand. But we caught up in the panic and although we tried to cling to each other, my hand slipped away. The next thing I knew, I was being led down a ladder into a lifeboat. The last thing I saw in the dark was the magnificent Titanic sinking into the dark waves below.

Samantha Earnshaw (12)
St Mary's RC High School, Hereford

A Day In The Life Of A Superstar

'And the winner is ... 'The Rockers!'

Hi, I'm Joe and I'm going to tell you the story of our success right from the beginning.

It all started one music lesson, when our teacher split us into groups. There were six of us; Me, Lucie, Fran, Pete, Joe and Kelly. We started with a basic idea and it expanded into something bigger and better.

I used to love it when it came to performing. We suddenly became the most popular people in the school. When we'd finished our piece everyone would clap, cheer, whoop and shout!

One day there was a visitor in school and he overheard us practising. It turned out he was the manager of a record company! I bet you can guess what happened next, that's right, we got a contract for a record studio!

What was big before turned into something even bigger, so that's how we ended up here, at the National Awards Stadium, collecting our trophy.

That's about the end of our story except we're still going to keep building on what we've done already and hopefully make ourselves known to the whole of England!

Frances Lloyd (11)
St Mary's RC High School, Hereford

A Day In The Life Of A Pair Of Very Expensive Shoes!

Friday 19th June 2005

'Beyoncé are you ready? Michelle and Kelly are waiting,' shouted the stage manager.

'No! I've got to put my shoes on.'

'That's my call,' I said.

The wardrobe door opened, she touched me, oh my God, oh my God, I think I'm having a panic attack! I can't do this, thousands of people are watching me!

'Ahhhhhhh,' the screaming fans were so loud. It hit me, not long ago I was being stitched together, now, oh no I think I'm going to faint, I feel really dizzy!

Snap went Beyoncé's heel. I collapsed, Beyoncé fell and hit the floor. People rushed over, they were running towards me. They were going to take me to people who fix shoes for celebrities, but they just undid me and threw me to the side. I felt used and unwanted. I decided to never work for celebrities ever again!

Antonia Morgan (12)
St Mary's RC High School, Hereford

A Day In The Life Of The Crazy Frog!

'Crazy Frog, hurry up you're going to be late for your new video shoot with Axel.'

'Coming now boss.' Anyway, where's my motorbike and my helmet? I'm not going to leap into action without having my stylish, cool, fantastic motorbike and helmet. Oh no, Axel is gigantic and has a robot face; that's so scary. I hope this doesn't take long.'

'Hello Crazy Frog, it will be a pleasure to work with you I'm sure. Anyway let's get on, the first scene we're doing is when you will be X-rayed and then jump off the hundred foot building.'

'I'm afraid nobody told me about that; do I really have to jump off a hundred foot building?'

'Yes you do, that's why we're paying you. Do you think we're paying you just to ride your invisible motorbike and your helmet? You must be crazzzzzzy.'

My gosh that man Axel is so moody, the next music video I'll be doing will hopefully be somebody like Eminem. That's likely, right Crazy Frog be cool, calm down; I'm cool and calm, let's go.

'One, two, three action.'

Oh no, I don't think I can do this ... one, two, three, here I go *wheeeee* ...

Rebecca Lovelock (12)
St Mary's RC High School, Hereford

A Day In The Life Of The Titanic

It was such a lovely day. People stared at me gasping at my vast luxurious figure.

Yes, I was the pride of England! Setting off on my maiden voyage. They named me the great Titanic! That name brought joy to my heart.

It had been a week or so of sailing happily flowing with calm waves of the cold Atlantic Ocean, when a sudden cold chill stung the air. We were reaching iceberg zone! A freezing mist settled so I couldn't see anything. It was so scary.

Being a ship (or a luxury liner as I call myself) is not fun. I don't get a second's rest, I have to just keep going! and my back aches terribly from all the people stamping, stomping, walking and running all over it day and night. Don't they think I tire of such reckless noises? Ohhh how my stomach groans from people slamming doors. Humph, didn't they think I had feelings?

Then I looked up and saw a jagged shape looming closer and closer in the mist ... What happened next was a mixture of confusion followed by panic. Screaming and crying by everyone on me. Then all went dark and quiet. I started to miss the happy laughter on board and the cleaners giving me a refreshing clean, but now there was no one to listen to.

Now 110 years on I tell the sad sale to all sea creatures passing by, wondering when they will raise me up to see the English sky.

Aniela Neicho (12)
St Mary's RC High School, Hereford

A Day In The Life Of A Tin Can

As a tin can I spend most of my time locked up high in a dark, dark cupboard. I wait and wait until a person opens the door of the cupboard and takes me out and looks at me. The person spins me in their hand and then sees my calories. I then often hear, 'Oh no, this is too fattening', or 'I'm not eating this!' I know I'm only a piece of scrap metal, but I do have feelings! The thought of chocolate spread and marmalade being taken out of the cupboard before me is like a supreme anger burning inside me wanting to lash out at everything.

I have been called 'Dog Waste', 'Mud Bucket', 'Cat Trap' and many other things. I suspect I deserve all these names being filled with mustard! I don't blame them for their actions, but I just wish I could travel from this dark cupboard onto better things. Oh well, just another day in the cupboard for me …

Johan van Meeuwen (12)
St Mary's RC High School, Hereford

A Day In The Life Of A Mobile Phone!

Oh no, here we go. Another day of hard work and pain. Right, my owner has woken up and he's yawning. Now he's got out of bed. He's standing up and walking over to the bathroom. The door's closed and the shower's on.

He's out of the shower and his suit is on. His hair is combed and his shoes are polished. He is ready. He picks me up and turns me on. The pain, the paaaiiinnn. Now he puts me in his pocket.

This is the boring bit of the day. No one ever rings because from eight in the morning until midday, my owner is always in board meetings. Should be called 'bored' meetings! At least it gives me a chance to brace myself for the frenzy to come.

Lunchtime is manic! Call after call after call, they all come in, and even I get sick and tired of my Crazy Frog tune. I get a headache from listening to my owner blab on about this and that, never mind the screeching voices of some of his friends. Just to add further suffering, he insists on texting at every available moment. Jab after jab, being prodded to death.

The afternoon passes fairly calmly, but the walk home is the dread of the day. We always pass the Vodaphone shop. It is full of shiny, flashing, metallic, brand spanking new phones. I am scared that one will catch his eye and I will be a gonna!

Alex Thomas (12)
St Mary's RC High School, Hereford

A Day In The Life Of Sylvia The Dragon

From the very start I knew that today was going to be a bad day. First of all, I woke up and realised that I had singed the floor (which is murder to get off, by the way). Then, I went over to the kitchen and there were no sheep, which meant that I had to go and round some more up as well as take the chicks to school, wash up and change the coal!

After all that I went to pick up the chicks and I was going to light a fire for dinner, until my chest packed up, so I had to rush to Mr Puff's to get a ready meal (which is highly unhealthy). We all ate that, then we had to go and bath Crystal and Gem and then put them to bed. Being over-excited, however, they didn't go to sleep until midnight.

With that busy day I only got time to fry 100 humans!

Rebecca Gilling (12)
St Mary's RC High School, Hereford

Wooden Terror

A dark forest frowned on either side of the frozen waterway. The trees had been stripped by a recent wind of their white covering of frost and they seemed to lean towards each other in the fading light.

The sharp wind picked up again and the forest was filled with a shade of winter. The leaves rustled in the gathering gloom and a noise rose through trees, hanging there like a heavy fog as the light flickered away.

The huddled men on the sides of the waterway froze, refusing to move in the wind. It was like a scene from a horror movie, like someone's there but you can't see them. Everything seemed to be trying to encase itself back in its own glass box. An old swing creaked back and forth in the wind. It seemed to creak a message, a warning.

I began to etch a path down the path and skidded and slipped onto the waterway next to the disused bridge. My heart was pounding inside my mouth and my stomach churned so hard it hurt. I slowly gathered myself together and stood on the ice.

A breath on my neck awoke my senses and I shot around looking for someone who seemed to be invisible. I turned again and there were gunshots, the snapping of leaves and a sharp crack like a whip, then a thud on the ice. I managed to let out one scream of despair before the whole world turned into darkness.

Catherine Leslie (13)
St Mary's RC High School, Hereford

My Last Day

Sunlight dances and sparkles on the fresh leaves; a disco of life. Through the trees my eyes transfix upon wild white stallions, pulling their lunar chariots with no effort, rising together to the base of a mountain. 300ft tall; aura of a king - this true leader commands a vast Roman empire. Its crater steams and bubbles, raging mildly at the pesky swallows. This volcano's jagged stone-aged knives tumble and turn; a presence within them to show their creator they can reach their eerie target - Pompeii.

That's where I live; 79AD. Father's a wine seller, I have to carry the ampullae from our room round the back, into their holes on the counter - they're heavy even without wine in! I usually get a coin for that. A bronze one with the Emperor's head on - the first coins. I didn't get a coin today because while jumping on the stones to the other side of the road on my way to Zeus' temple, I slipped and covered my toga in sewage and almost got run over by a chariot.

I'm in a sulk today because my favourite gladiator is fighting a strange animal over the sea from Africa called a rhinoceros (supposedly it's got a horn!). Anyway it costs three coins for coliseum entrance, so I need the money.

In the baths now, the steam pool relaxes me and the bright mosaics cheer me, but today I can't relax, I keep hearing rumblings from Zeus knows where. Is that human screams?

Eva Howard (13)
St Mary's RC High School, Hereford

Hungry Poverty

Many people don't know the meaning of hunger. Yet I do. My mum had died in childbirth; my baby sister too. My dad was involved in the civil war and he died - shot twice in the left arm and then stabbed. So nowadays it was just me and my brother.

We had no home to live in. We had no clothes to change into. We had no food to eat. All we had left were each other and in my mind all I could see were people in prosperous countries, such as England and America, eating masses, throwing out any leftovers and not thinking about us - the poor and needy.

Looking up I could see military aeroplanes, gunfire ringing and remnants shattering, soaring down to my feet. This was nothing out of the ordinary, but we would have to find refuge, otherwise we would be captured; killed.

My brother and I ran, dodging all of the falling dust and random gunfire. However, the day was hot and the ground sun dry. Our rags were sweaty, torn, filthy from the daily wear and tear. Our legs were too weak to run fast, our arms floppy and lifeless and our stomachs hungry and empty. We had no energy. We had no life. The effort of living was too tiring and nobody would make it easier for us. Nobody cared or they would do something for us and prevent the amount of poverty that is arising in this world.

Kimberley Langford (13)
St Mary's RC High School, Hereford

A Day In The Life Of Rose Sharp

Dear Diary,

Today was horrible. I hate being the daughter of a rich mum, who is posh and no one can stand! I guess you want to know what happened today.

It all started out normal, Karry (our servant) came to wake me up and dress me.

'Wake up,' she said.

'OK,' I replied.

She just stared at me and then said, 'I am here to dress you.'

'How many times, I'm not a kid!'

'OK and it is child not kid,' she said.

When I was ready, Mother told me we were going on an outing. I couldn't believe it, she never took me out!

While I was having breakfast Angus, our chef, came out and said, 'Are you looking forward to today?'

That minute Mother flew down the stairs and said, 'John just called, I am going to a party!'

'But Mum,' I moaned.

'No, Mother,' she said. Mother didn't care about our trip she was so wrapped up about the party.

With that I stormed up the stairs and put my jacket on.

As I was going out the door Mother shouted, 'Go play with your friends.'

'I don't have any friends thanks to you!' I slammed the door and went outside.

All of the children looked at me and whispered about me, I felt like an animal in the zoo. Everyone had friends apart from me and it was all my mother's fault, so that is why I had a rotten day!

Harriet Chapman (12)
St Mary's RC High School, Hereford

The Legend Of The Beasts

Long ago, when there was no gunpowder, there lived a man, this man was called Ohginum, he lived in a little village called Bonba.

When he was 61 the black beast came and many people died but he became stronger and stronger ...

People started saying that he was a demon because it looked like he became younger every day.

He went to the mountains with his wife, Strania. In there he lived off bats and some other animals, he lived in a 'cage' as his wife called it but it was a cave.

Then somehow his wife got pregnant, having 3 boys. They called them, Them, Themus and Themulus.

They went to the village when they were bigger to get food for their father (Mum had died) but on a full moon night two of those sons were bitten, one by a bat and one by a wolf, and then it happened.

Them, who was bitten by a bat, became a creature called 'vampire' and Themulus became a werewolf.

Themus wasn't bitten but got married so he became a real human, but what would happen if he was bitten by a wolf and a bat? Would he become a vampire, a werewolf or both?

Fábio Anselmo (12)
St Mary's RC High School, Hereford

The Sandy Desert

Thunder and lightning lashed on to the sandy desert. Rain filled the empty sky with dark, depressing clouds.

Children ran from parks and gardens. Empty swings squeaked as they swung from side to side. The sandcastles melted into the sandpit becoming part of the desert.

As night-time came the storms became worse. The sound of doors being locked, children screaming from nightmares and the pitter-patter of tiny feet clambering into their parents' bed because the loud thunder and bright lightning could be heard.

The lightning struck the sand leaving a circle of glowing sand. Waves of heat rose from the glowing object. Most people don't know this, but when lightning strikes sand that is dug up when cool it turns into a magnificent glass object.

Rachel Ingram (14)
St Mary's RC High School, Hereford

Cats Grow Fins!

There has been a record decrease in fish populations as the first family of artificially bred cats has taken to the water. These cats have been given gills and fins to help them hunt.

Could this be the end of the land-water barrier that has been hindering us for millennia? We asked the scientist who is in charge of this project, Peter McFishy, to give us some details at a recent press conference: 'These cats have been bred to breathe in water without surfacing to surprise fish. They can also breathe in the normal way to hunt on land'.

When asked about cats hating water, we were told: 'People have always believed that cats hate water but we believe that cats can be trained to like it. We have, from birth, put them in an environment where they are close to water and they seem to be happy about swimming now'. The company who bred these cats have no intention of releasing them into the wild, instead they will keep them in a zoo with other animals which they have created. These will include a singing hippo and a pink rhinoceros.

'This zoo will be a thing to remember,' said Mrs Miggins, a pie shop owner who has bought a stand at the new zoo. 'My pies will be the highlight of people's day here. The animals are just a side attraction'.

Tickets are expected to cost around £10 for adults and £7 for concessions.

Lloyd Collins (13)
St Mary's RC High School, Hereford

Breakers

From where I stand I can see to either end of the beach, its wet sand glimmering underneath my feet, reflecting the moon. There's something about tonight that makes me stay, even after the others have left. Something plays on the sea breeze and makes up my mind to reside there.

The scene is beautiful; rolling waves crashing up onto the shore then dissolving away, sinking back to the sea. Snow-white sand glistens with the remnants of a high tide that has been and passed. It is littered with tiny pebbles and shells that gleam as stars on the shore, reflecting the moon. And it's all framed by dark, picturesque cliffs on either side …

But suddenly, the sea becomes rougher, the waves swirling up into great mounds of water, twice as high as they were before. Breakers surge powerfully up onto the beach and all the while I am standing at the shoreline, watching. Somehow I know that I'm safe. Looking out over the sea as it wrestles itself endlessly I have to blink then look again. No, it's not my imagination; they're really there …

Hundreds of ivory-white horses gallop towards me, riding the swell. Magnificent forelegs plunge in and out of the water, opulent manes flay out along their necks and deep, sapphire-blue eyes are set regally in their heads. They are awe-inspiring.

They look so real. They're fictional and yet here they are, so close I feel I could touch them. I wish I could touch them … I wish …

Mollie Russell (12)
St Mary's RC High School, Hereford

Running Away

I hated the way they treated me, as if I were dirt, I was just the little girl in the corner, the little girl who could be used for anything, to look after the younger children or to clean the house, even to cook the dinner. I was sick of them, I hated them and now they had to live without me, I was running away from the hurt, from the danger, from the family that never wanted me.

They were all watching the TV, laughing at something inappropriate once again. Now was the perfect time, I ran up to my small, dark bedroom and packed the few clothes I had into a small bag full of holes. I crept into my little brothers' room, they were both asleep, little Sammy in his cradle and Timmy lying in his bed, tears started trickling down my eyes. I loved these two boys as much as anything in the world and it was heartbreaking how I was leaving them with these people. I bent down and kissed them both on the forehead and whispered goodbye. Slowly I tiptoed down the stairs and into the kitchen, I grabbed some food and took the money from my piggy bank, which I had been saving up. Now it was my turn for an opportunity, for a chance to live my life the way it should have been. I opened the old wooden door and I was gone into the darkness, into my own world.

Julianne Clark (13)
St Mary's RC High School, Hereford

Winda The Goddess Of Wind

In the early time of the gods, there was a god or goddess for each wind. Every day, depending how Zeus was feeling, he would choose a gust, breeze, gale etc. However he was a happy man so he used the breezes and gusts most. This caused Galea, Tornada and Hurrican to become jealous.

The gods and goddesses had sworn on their lives never to kill another god or goddess. However jealousy and hatred for Gusto and Breez had forced the others to take action. From that day onward there was always fighting between the two groups, each planning attacks and using other gods and goddesses for spies. Both sides tried to make Zeus use their wind but none succeeded.

As each year came and went Zeus got more and more fed up with the feud, so finally he called a conference and they all met at his palace. Zeus and the other gods had had enough! They had come up with an idea; all they had to do was get permission from the wind gods and goddesses.

Their idea was; all the gods and goddesses of the wind were to become one, so that there would be no more arguing. The new goddess was to be called Winda and would control all the types of wind. Everything was fine, except for one thing, Galea, Tornada and Hurrican still hadn't agreed. After much persuading and reasoning they agreed, the problem was solved and Winda was born.

Isabel Fawcett (12)
St Mary's RC High School, Hereford

Tales

As Prometheus struggled vainly at his chains, an eagle leapt out of its eyrie and flew down to its supper ... Prometheus.

'Keith,' hailed Prometheus as the eagle ruffled its wings and bent down to the job it was sent to do. Writhing, Prometheus gasped as Keith ripped his flesh, 'You don't have to do this, you know,' he pleaded.

'Oh yeah. Why not?'

'Don't you get bored of liver?'

Keith shrugged, 'I like it.'

Prometheus dropped his voice conspiratorially, 'Zeus is really punishing you. He saw that the eagles were getting smarter than he was, so he sent off the most intelligent, that's you, to be punished.'

Keith preened his feathers - he liked being flattered, 'You think so?'

'I know so, Zeus is a traitor, terrified that someone might get the power to overthrow him.'

'Really?' Keith was interested now, all thoughts of food forgotten. But before Prometheus could answer a voice boomed around the mountain.

'How dare you? This is a disgrace to all deities!' Zeus floated down on to the rock. Keith fled in terror. 'You gave the humans fire against my orders and now you tell tales to my faithful servants - the eagles, so be it, I condemn you to spend the rest of eternity in the tongues of humans forcing them to tell tales and lies and they will curse your name a thousand times over before their age is done!'

So that was how humans came to tell tales and lies, it wasn't our fault at all.

Josie Walters (13)
St Mary's RC High School, Hereford

A Day In The Life Of A Roman Soldier

The mud made a squelch under our feet as we moved through the boggy wetland, the heather growing on either side with its pink flowers soon to be blood-soaked. On a hill just above where we were standing you could make out hordes of barbarians ready to be destroyed by our mastery of warfare. Their men didn't scare us. The only advantage they had accumulated was that they were on a slight incline. We though had superiority. Were they about to surrender like the war-torn grass that surrendered to war?

Then dramatically from the hilltop they came rushing down. The front ranks bracing themselves bringing their bloodstained swords out of their holders and pushing the shields out in front to absorb the blow. Down they tumbled from the hill, endless masses of ill-equipped men ready to be slaughtered. I thrust my shield into them knocking three or four unconscious and then began to slice without knowing what I was doing. The smell of blood clouded the air and the sunlight was blocked by the clouds of arrows gleaming ready to kill whoever they hit. Another charge and more dead but only a few of our men fell in the endless onslaught that we had to endure.

Then suddenly the ranks broke. Hundreds of barbarians fleeing to the hills and then we saw it, their leader had died, we had won, the British hillside back under our control. We knew though that their challenge was not over.

Adam Powell (13)
St Mary's RC High School, Hereford

Tales

Cobwebs adorned with spiders like tiny jewels drifted sinisterly in the breeze. The thick masses of trees creaked and stretched their weary limbs, seeming almost alive in their lust for movement. An air of sleepless menace shadowed over the land swallowing the air and leaving behind a nauseating stench that paralysed both man and beast.

But you strode on, disbelieving the old tales of magic and danger, dismissing them as fairy tales and unproven myths. You brushed aside the cobwebs, leaving tiny spiders to scuttle into holes in the ground, you kicked aside the toadstools and spat on the tiny hoards of fungi that wove their way up delicate tree trunks.

The trees had begun to whisper, to crackle their leaves in anger, stirring up the evil that had grown there many years before.

You walked on, blaspheming the gods and fairies that we knew only too well existed. You reached a pool, a magical pool, dark and depthless. You threw stones, you broke the surface, you disturbed the hidden water.

Then suddenly, there were paw prints, paw prints that hadn't been there before. The air grew tight almost like magic which didn't exist in your mind. Yet what was the warmth on your neck and the ripples of the pool that had appeared out of nowhere … ?

We heard you scream though we heard nothing else. No word from the old forest, no cries for help, no breath, no wail. You should have believed the old tales, you should never have entered in there.

Amber Gray (12)
St Mary's RC High School, Hereford

How Biker Babe Got Her Name

There was a man long ago who lived in Manchester. He was a salesman and sold everything bar the kitchen sink.

He decided to go to watch the motorbike races. He would make a lot of money selling his things there. Everyone in Manchester loved going to see the bikes racing.

The bikes sped past him, some yellow, some green, some red and some black. 'These bikes are wicked man, they go so fast don't they?' asked a stranger to the salesman but he didn't answer. 'They're wicked ain't they mate? They go so fast don't they?' But the salesman still did not answer. 'Oi, are you listening or not? If you don't answer me I'll punch you!' said the stranger.

'Well my girlfriend can drive faster than those bikes, they go well slow compared to her!' answered the salesman.

'Yeah, well bring her here tomorrow and then we'll see who's faster. If you're lying to me I'll smash your face in.'

The salesman's girlfriend wasn't very happy about this arrangement. She wasn't feeling very well and didn't want to start racing people for her boyfriend's safety. Even though she didn't want to do it she went to bed and slept till her alarm went off.

When they got to the track everyone was a bit stressed.

'Three races,' declared the judges, 'best of three.'

They set off. She won the first. Oh yeah, the second and the third. She was the champ. As she walked back to collect her trophy she heard the crowd, they chanted, 'Biker Babe,' as loud as they could. *That shall be my name,* she thought and from then on to this day she has been known as Biker Babe.

Eve Grisenthwaite (13)
St Mary's RC High School, Hereford

The Horse Whisperer

A horse whisperer, myth or reality? Some people believe, some of them don't. One girl didn't believe any of this then something happened that changed her whole life forever.

Faith arrived at her friend Hannah's house. Hannah was her normal cheerful self. Hannah invited her into her room, she had a surprise to show her. Faith wondered what the surprise could be. Hannah got out a box; inside the box were tarot cards. Hannah said she would read Faith her future. Hannah placed five cards on the bed and told Faith what they meant.

'Faith, the cards tell me your future will be with animals, you will become a horse whisperer.'

'What!' Faith replied. 'How can that be? I hate horses!'

This troubled Faith a lot. Hannah could see this, so she took Faith outside and they walked into a field that was a short distance from the house. 'Look,' Hannah pointed. In the field was a chestnut horse. 'Go and see him,' Hannah forced.

Faith didn't want to, so Hannah pushed her into the field. Faith slowly walked towards the animal, as she got nearer she sensed the horse was hurting, she saw the horse was hurting. But Hannah didn't seem to think that he was hurt. This confused her. But then she realised she had the powers of a horse whisperer. Faith now understood and realised her gift, that she had to help horses. The horses needed her like she now needed the horses.

Victoria Westbrook (13)
St Mary's RC High School, Hereford

Fear

Ten minutes away from the park my heart was already pounding in my chest. I have always liked theme parks but I have never been one for big, fast rides. This theme park had them all. It wasn't meant for kids. Today was going to be the day I was to confront my fear of heights by going on the biggest ride of all; Oblivion. Standing at a height of 11ft in the air with a vertical drop, it was *not* going to be easy.

The queues were exhausting in themselves; they were particularly long leading to Oblivion, but being as nervous as me, every minute felt like a lifetime. My heart was pounding faster, louder, harder, it felt like it was going to leap out of my chest, I became very hot, pale and I felt faint, but I had to do this; it was going to be the experience of a lifetime and I couldn't let my fear of heights tear me away from it.

Up at the top, the tension was indescribable, in a few seconds time I would be down on the ground again. In a few seconds it would be all over. *Drop!* My stomach was in my mouth, it was like nothing I had ever felt in my life before.

Back on the ground again I felt overwhelmed, I had done it! My friend asked to do it again! Disappointing her I took a deep breath and said, 'Never again.'

Lindsey Haile (14)
St Mary's RC High School, Hereford

The Invisible Beast

The invisible beast sweeps through the woodland as a bird swoops through the heavens. The invisible beast leaves the dew in the daybreak and the stars in the twilight. The invisible beast commences the sunrise and abolishes the sundown. The invisible beast appears every night to present us with our dreams. The invisible beast is the originator of our Earth. The invisible beast will one day conclude our spirit and will impel us to another world, where we shall inaugurate our existence yet again. The invisible beast furnishes us with the exemption to independence and liberation of speeding. The invisible beast is always there for us and is awaiting our visit to him to observe any dilemmas we may have. The invisible beast will outlive us all.

The invisible beast is propounding us with his hand to superintend us on the correct way to peace and happiness.

The invisible beast is God.

Charlotte Baggott (14)
St Mary's RC High School, Hereford

The Knife

I'm sitting here waiting. *But am I waiting for my girlfriend Sadie or am I waiting for something to fulfil me?* I keep spinning those questions round in my head; to try and straighten it all out, to try and make some sense. I feel pain tugging on my heartstrings, worse than ever before. I just want to curl up and let it go.

I'm sitting on a battered swing in a very gloomy park. The slide and pole rusting into nothingness and the wooden frames have been stripped down to its bare bones. The grass is dead and the only living things out here are the trees, who whisper in hushed voices. Everything around me is looking straight through me, knowing my deepest secrets, knowing every thought that passes my mind.

I look up to the already half-covered moon, its dim glow lighting up the park. *What is that?* I hear a rustle of leaves. Is it Sadie? I feel a rise of hope fill up inside me. Then a strange bent over figure appears before me. Now the hope is replaced by terror. What does this man want? Does he even know that I'm here? My hand brushes against my pocket. I feel my trusting knife.

The moon is hidden, leaving the park in darkness. I just want to get out of here! Then I hear it. I hear Sadie's voice call my name. I stop but I can't think straight. Oh Sadie where are you?

Jessica Rivers (14)
St Mary's RC High School, Hereford

How The World Lost Its Beauty

After the beginning, when all the gods had done their deeds, when Epimetheus and Prometheus had made all the living creatures, after Venus had added her beauty and Athena had offered her wisdom the world was no longer an empty atmosphere, soil was rich in minerals. Darkness did not exist. Everyone was equal and the kingdom was ruled by the gods.

Meanwhile, the wicked Lord of the Underworld, Hades, saw what was happening and soon grew jealous of the new world. With one quick swipe the Eden could have disappeared but Hades wanted to hurt the gods another way.

He crept into the paradise world and stole a single rose petal. For months and months he worked hard moulding that single rose petal into an elegant young woman. When all was complete and the woman shone with beauty Hades named her Evangeline. However, unlike her beauty, Hades gave her all his qualities, jealousy, selfishness, greed, vanity and more.

When all was complete and Evangeline was perfect in every evil way she was placed on Earth.

Soon every man fell under her spell and twins were born but sadly they inherited their mother's genes.

Soon they had twins and they had twins and so on until the whole world was full of Hades' wicked qualities. Nothing was ever the same again.

Roisin Richards (14)
St Mary's RC High School, Hereford

The Chase

It was a night like no other. The darkness pressed in like a ravaging beast and the blue moon hung in the sky. The only sign of life on the darkened world was a young boy, running for his life. His straw-blond hair was drenched with sweat which stuck to his pale face. There were cuts over his face where the brambles had clung at him and he clutched his arm to stem the flow of blood from a deep gash, the mark was from the foul beast that was in pursuit.

The form this pet of Satan took was that of a black horse, with a mane of iron and eyes of fire.

As the boy fled he heard the sound of the thunderous hooves of the horse drawing ever closer, then he felt the steed of the Devil upon him. It jumped with ease over the fleeing figure and blocked his path forward, it turned its fiery eyes upon the boy who felt a move of icy terror erupt inside him. The more the boy looked into the horse's eyes, the weaker he felt, until he collapsed on the ground, shrivelled and soulless.

James North (14)
St Mary's RC High School, Hereford

A Day In The Life Of A Not So Ordinary Girl

As usual I started my day with breakfast, eating my soggy cornflakes at the table next to my stepbrother and stepfather as my mum makes their breakfasts because they're too lazy to do it themselves. It's as if I'm Cinderella only with a wicked stepbrother and stepfather. They make me do all their chores (it's not like I don't have my own).

Anyway, my day was different to any usual day. I went back to my bedroom after breakfast and something magnificent happened as I was holding in my stress with tears, forcing myself not to scream and shout at how much I hate my life. I found out that I have a gift, a special gift that no one would ever believe. I can become invisible!

After finding out this gift I decided not to tell anyone, not even Mum. I wouldn't want her to think I'm crazy but the one person I could trust would be my best friend, Isabella. I thought I should tell her at school, the one place where I like to be!

As I stepped out of the front door my stepfather started shouting at me screaming, 'You're not getting a lift to school, you can walk, you haven't ironed my work clothes.' I couldn't believe it, he still had to take Jake to school, but mostly I couldn't believe my mum didn't stick up for me, she just sat there. Sometimes I think she's under a spell or something! From now on my life shall be different!

Hannah Butterfield (14)
St Mary's RC High School, Hereford

A Day In The Life Of An Iraqi

Dear Journal,

They're still here. They prowl the streets spreading paranoia and causing pandemonium. No longer do we feel safe on the streets of our home. The men came promising freedom but all they gave to us was curfews and restrictions. They have killed thousands of innocent civilians (like my brother) with their inaccurate scatter bombs. They also have taken our oil, which we need for our whole economy to survive. They say they have given us democracy but all the candidates were chosen by them. No matter who you voted for, you were really just voting for them. They say they are a 'coalition of freedom', but they are really a 'coalition of oppression and misery'. They even break international rules of war by torturing our brave soldiers. They not only torture but they mock as well. They take pictures of the poor men stripped and make them pose in several very disgusting positions.

Finally they even call our courageous freedom fighters an evil and horrible word, 'terrorists'. This really makes me want to join the freedom fighters, for they are the terrorists invading our country and throwing down our leader. I've even found out that in their country they are seen as heroes. All of this hatred and violence toward their fellow man makes you wonder. What is the world coming to?

Nathan Longworth (13)
St Mary's RC High School, Hereford

Just Another Statistic

The day was beautiful. The sun shone brightly, the grass swayed in the cool breeze. I laid back and closed my eyes, I felt Jason lie down next to me, his arms holding me in a tight embrace. Opening my eyes I gazed into his handsome face. Propping myself up on one elbow I leaned in close to his ear and whispered, 'I love you.' My heart stopped as I waited for his reply, gazing deep into his hazel eyes.

'I love you too,' he whispered and holding hands like we would never let go, we kissed as though to seal the agreement of everlasting love.

But that was before the letter came. The letter that threatened to destroy our love. But even though all the odds were against us, love shone through and waving goodbye I knew he would come back. He had to. Days passed, then weeks and then came a knock at the door. The solemn faces, the apologies. His death just another statistic, the death of my one true love just a mark on a piece of paper somewhere. All I have now are bittersweet memories to take with me through life.

Lauren Phillips (13)
St Mary's RC High School, Hereford

Supreme God

'The only one true god', the Romans called him.

'The one who keeps Hell's door shut and brings forever light,' the Greeks said.

'The child of the Earth, Father of the Nile,' the Egyptians proclaimed.

He is said to have had created Heaven, a strong kingdom never to let Hell through. He alone holds the black gates shut. This supreme god is the father, also for the Norse god, Odin and the Greek god, Zeus the once named 'all fathers'.

He is able to make the Devil himself shiver in fear of his tremendous power: casting seeds from Heaven to the ground-making forests grow and being able to destroy cities with a touch of his finger.

He creates all these natural disasters that have ever happened in the world, the tsunami in 2004, the tornado in USA in 1931 and the earthquake in Turkey in ancient times.

You may say that he is evil and unforgiving but without him we would have no Earth, sun and no life.

Joshua Lambert (13)
St Mary's RC High School, Hereford

A Day In The Life Of A Survivor

I violently grabbed for the surface, whilst my legs tangled in the murky, green seaweed, my arms flailing helplessly, I was trapped, a prisoner held captive. The strong current taking me from side to side. I felt like a small kitten drowning in a downpour of rain, I clawed for the surface, each time getting closer.

I hit the surface panting heavily. I fought against the chaotic waves. After what felt like hours and hours I reached land. Whilst hauling myself to the rough sand, my limbs weak, I collapsed. The dark, depressing coldness escaped me and the bright sun pounded at my body, as if I were in a raging fire. I looked to the deep blue ocean, so peaceful now, so beautiful, yet dangerous.

Still gasping, I laid down on the tiny, microscopical particles beneath me, in a daze, I thought of the others and I drifted off into the pleasant spell of unconsciousness, the faint breeze brushing past my weathered face, clinging to the hope, the hope that there might be others like me, other survivors.

Lauren Kedward (12)
St Mary's RC High School, Hereford

What Happened Next, The Landlady

'So there's been no one staying here in three years apart from Mr Mulholland, Mr Temple and I?' Billy questioned in disbelief.

'No, absolutely no one,' replied the landlady.

'How strange,' said Billy.

'Hope you don't mind me asking but why do you have so many books on medicines and experiments on that bookshelf?' asked Billy wandering over.

'Mr … Mr Weaver, it's just, um, an interest of mine,' she stuttered.

'I'm interested in medicines myself, may I look at some books?' he questioned.

'They're of no use, they're old now,' she asserted. Billy still opened a book somewhere near the middle, wiping dust off the page with his hand. The landlady quickly walked over to Billy, clutching more tea. Billy took the cup from the unsteady hand of the old woman, took a sip then put it down. He closed the book slowly, letting the pages brush against his fingertips.

Did that say almonds? thought Billy, violently turning back pages. 'Page 27, almond poison'. Billy tasted the flavour in his mouth then ran to find a bathroom. He tried not to swallow the contents in his mouth. Bursting into a room, he spluttered the tea out on the floor.

He stood bolt upright, it was sickening, Mr Mulholland and Mr Temple's dead bodies. Hearing the pitter-patter of the landlady's slippers on the stairs, he attempted to run away …

It was an accident, he barged into her and she fell down the stairs, lying as motionless as the bodies. He was just as guilty as she was. Billy strolled to the bookshelf, page 27, almond poison …

Georgina Lawrence (14)
St Mary's RC High School, Hereford

Angel Alice

The lightning crashed on the outback of the charcoal-black hills. Rain splattered onto the thirsty earth as the heavens opened. Soldiers poured out of the rapidly collapsing trenches. Bodies lay in a sea of red dirt as the hungry rats gorged upon their rotting corpses. Gunshots echoed this world. The Earth is owned by fire, blazing, smoking, creeping up on innocent people to die a long and painful death. Light flashes and crashes into a swirling man-made storm, torturing and destroying every natural and beautiful thing in its desolate path. I fear for my mortal family. I fear for my friends who are alive and well. I fear for every wonderful person on this planet of chaos.

A man curls his small and frail body into the corner of a trench full of disease and faeces. He unfolds a crumpled piece of paper and receives the joyful news that his wife has given birth to a beautiful baby boy. The soldier would never see this beautiful, bouncy, blue-eyed baby. This Earth has turned into a world of torment and evil. Earth is now Hell. Watching civilisation grow to love and care for each other. Watching children laugh. Watching generosity spread through the love in this hungry land. My spirit is still with my people. My soul reaches out and warms their hearts with the love from mine as the wind whispers … 'Angel Alice is here' …

Georgina Edgar (14)
St Mary's RC High School, Hereford

A Day In The Life Of A Lion At The Zoo

I yawned as the sun crept through my cage. Siân, the other lion in my cage was pacing up and down the grimy window that looks out of our small, dirty cage. She was trying to find a way out, that's what she spent the majority of each day doing. I didn't understand her; there clearly wasn't a way out. It was just a waste of time. Unlike her I spent most of the day sunbathing. I winced and saw some visitors arriving. It was yet another boring day of annoying children banging and shouting at our window trying to get us to move.

In the wild you can roam around freely, catch fresh meat and eat whenever you want. In the zoo your every move is watched, you don't get a choice of food, just whatever. Dry, old meat is chucked to you and worse still; there are no animals to chase, so you don't get an exhilarating feeling. I hate the zoo. Have humans ever thought if we liked it? We are living creatures too. How would they like it if their privacy and freedom were taken away? They would most definitely despise it.

Allegra Fowler-Wright (12)
St Mary's RC High School, Hereford

A Day In The Life Of Bombing

Bombs shatter houses like glass. Sirens scream in my ears, waking me up, warning me I'm no longer safe. I jump out of bed, putting on my gas mask.

Rushing downstairs I collect my parcel and run straight to the Anderson shelter at the bottom of the garden. It's the fourth raid this week and I'm getting used to the wailing of my sister when my parents get in the shelter. It's starting to seem compulsory. I'm beginning to handle being locked in the dank darkness of the shelter confined to a few feet. It's beginning to look and feel quite homely.

My dad's taught me that if you listen carefully to when a bomb's dropped and start counting elephants once you manage to reach eight you're safe. I wonder why it's elephants, why not chickens or sheep? Dad says it's got something to do with counting out accurate seconds. I hear a bomb being set free and I begin to count one elephant, two elephants, three elephants, four elephants, five elephants, six elephants, seven elephants, eight elephants. Phew we made it! I try to fall asleep, I can't deal with all the tension but I'm not tired any more, I have to stick it out. I can't deal with all the wailing. If I have to wait out another bomb again I'll take Dad's pistol to my head! Here we go again, another bomb starts falling, one elephant, two elephants, three elephants, four elephants, five elephants, six elephants, seven elephants ...

Laura Jones (13)
St Mary's RC High School, Hereford

A Day In The Life Of My Dog Alfie

I am woken up by dogs barking. This is my cue to get up and wait for my family. I patiently sit next to the door, ready for them to let me out. I stand up as I hear them coming. The door opens and there is my favourite master smiling at me. I get very excited and wagging my tail I run and jump up on him. He stumbles back a little bit.

I run onto the sofa, snuggling myself into a ball, covering my cold nose. My master sits next to me having his breakfast. Yummy! I love crumpets. I put on my 'cute' face which always works and he gives in. I then go back to sleep.

My master shouts, 'Walkies.' I love going for walks as I can run around barking and playing. We always jog down the hill. I then see another dog!

I run as fast as I can towards the dog. When my leash clicks and I stumble over I think it's a game and start biting my leash. My master starts playing with me as well.

When we come back home I am starving! I dash to my food bowl and guzzle it down. I have a quick drink then run to my master.

We spend the rest of the day playing tug-of-war, fetch and wrestling. I love it!

Soon I get tired, so I snuggle up to my master and fall asleep; dreaming of the exciting day we've had together.

Daniel Stamp (14)
St Mary's RC High School, Hereford

Fortunate Flight

I pressed my sweat-drenched palm against the door and drew it back hastily thinking what to do. I can't get out this way and I'm two floors up. How am I going to get out? My breath increased sharply, my lungs taking in air as fast as it went out. My mind turned to my family. Was Mum alright? Was Dad? I began to feel the heat in the room and smoke began to seep through the gap in the door. I glanced around sharply, trying to find a possible solution for this mess. I was doomed! Fourteen years of education and all I could come up with is: I'm doomed.

Interrupting my train of doom-like thought the fire decided it was to solve my dilemma and with a huge groan the floor; with as little warning as a thief in a dark alley, gave way.

The fall which was suddenly halted by a cushioning sofa; mentally jolted me and left me momentarily dazed. Eyes watering however I quickly noticed my situation and realised the room was thick with smoke that I couldn't have cut through with a knife.

I created a mental map of the room and felt for the direction the sofa was pointing, since this would lead to the window. Coughing like an asthmatic life-time smoker, I stumbled in the appropriate direction and felt the cool breeze momentarily causing me to forget the raging fire around me. I took my luck and leapt into the breeze and landed to my relief on a soft patch of grass, taking in a deep breath of full rich air. I, to my relief returned to my slumber.

Chris Davies (14)
St Mary's RC High School, Hereford

A Day In The Life Of ...

Thousands of miles away from my native land - I long to return. I battle to keep my tenacious place, marching across yards of dry, perished land. Ruined land. The majestic sunshine sucks me into her destructive atmosphere. After eight months here I am feeling the undeniable fatigue of eight years. I have trashed three of Saddam Hussein's squalid palaces - smashed the brightly polished porcelain frame that held the glossy photo of the man himself. Each single piece splattering across the marble interiors remains a memoir of broken civilisations. A broken country. I long for night's bitter blanket to pour over the sizzling skies.

The heat conjures up automatic chaos. A realistic bang shudders through the lifeless dense air. A bomb. My march quickens to a terrifying run as I hear tragic cries slice through the sunburnt air, *Nar, nar.* Fire. Spitting and hissing through the hot summer's air as it unveils its most deadly weapon. Death. The ever burning rubble is anger. The unbearable, victimising heat is terrorism. Victims of this ruthless brutality are retrieved out of the blazing inferno. Laying the dead to rest will never overcome the unstoppable anger the damaged society of Iraq carry for eternities after eternities. Crowds gather around the lifeless rubble. Anger spreads uncontrollably through the crowds like soldiers marching an infinite route. Extinguish a fire but you will never extinguish this gathering storm of anger that gradually builds to the very end.

Linda Bairkdar (14)
St Mary's RC High School, Hereford

A Day In the Life Of Frank White

To my dearest Violet,
    Today was another false alarm! Everybody was asleep when … the alarm went off. Well I've been thinking about you and baby Gary and I thought up a poem that might put your worries to rest:

> I say it was a shocking sight,
> The battlefield was alight.
> For many thousand bodies here
> Lay rotting in the sun;
> But things like that, you know, we must have *won!*
> Because it was the other team that was rotting in the sun!

Love your sweet husband, Frank.

Jayne Sargent (12)
St Mary's RC High School, Hereford

Murder Mystery

Around about 10pm our journey was about to begin. We were on a boat owned by Andy and Liam, we had been invited to join them on their holiday. I was not suspicious but afterwards I was very much so. Everybody had gone to sleep except me, Andy and Liam. Bob and Sam were tired and slept most of the trip. At 6am we arrived at our destination.

On the dock the sweltering heat was unbearable, we rushed for our hotel. There were not a lot of people around. Andy and Liam owned one of the villas in the hotel, they were very generous in letting us stay and we were very grateful. The villa was perfect, all the objects inside and outside were placed exactly in the right place.

Three hours later, Bob and Sam decided to go to a nightclub. Again I was with Andy and Liam, but soon enough both of them went out. Liam went to a bar while Andy went off alone.

Meanwhile I decided to go out for a stroll on the beach. A couple of party-like hours later we were all back resting in the villa (everyone except Bob).

Sam appeared upset over something, in fact she looked distraught. I tried to comfort and ask her about the reason she was crying. She was making some kind of signal to me by blinking her eyes reasonably fast. We walked outside and she revealed the horrible truth - Andy had murdered Bob.

I did not react. I felt sick. The murderer of my best friend was living with me for a week. I thought we should stay and try and find out why he'd committed the murder.

The next day we all went to watch a cricket match, West Indies Vs Australia. We all enjoyed it. Sam chose to have another walk, this time she did not return.

The following morning we discovered her washed up on the beach. She had stab wounds throughout her body. I was all alone. I needed help.

Soon my wishes were granted, a detective arrived in an unusual fashion …

Matthew Appleby & Liam Commins
Sherwood Hall School & Sixth Form College, Mansfield

The Diary Of My Budgerigar

7.30am 'Aw, what's the matter now? Let me go back to sleep.'
The budgie's owner turns the light on, it is 7.30am - time to get up. The budgie begins to squawk like mad but eventually calms down.

8.26am 'Hey, where are you going? Come and play with me. Oh well, if you insist on leaving me, I might as well have my breakfast.'
The owner is leaving for school. The budgie will spend some quality time on its own - even if it objects at first. 8.26am is breakfast and nothing can turn a budgie away from its food.

12.13pm 'Hmm, what shall I do? I know, I'll have a light snack.'
As I said, budgies love food. It is 12.13pm, a perfect time for the budgie to tuck into its seed dish - yum!

3.38pm 'Hey, where did you come from? Do you want to listen to me sing? *La, la, la.*'
The budgie's owner has arrived from school. Budgies love companionship, so the budgie will just sit and watch its owner doing housework. It may sound boring but that's a budgie's way of life.

10.01pm 'Oi, where did you go? I can't see anything. I'm blind, ahh. I'm so tired, maybe I'll just have a quick nap ...'
It is the budgie's bedtime. In the morning its adventure will begin all over again.

Amy Pearson (14)
Sherwood Hall School & Sixth Form College, Mansfield

A Day In The Life Of A Swift

It was the last day in September and the weather was getting rather cool. I had lived in a barn in the middle of Scotland during the summer and early spring. It was quite handy to share my barn with the cows because of all the flies they attracted. I dipped and dived, catching them all day and then at night slept in a nest I had made during the spring.

It's great being one of the fastest and smallest birds around, I can get to places quickly and squeeze in almost anywhere, but like everything I do there are disadvantages, like being chased by bigger birds. Anyway, because the weather was getting cooler, I had to migrate to South America because I get too cold in the winter around here. I made a meal of some flies and set off, passing and flying over houses, factories, shops and all kinds of buildings. I was flying through chimney smoke that was making me feel sick and making it difficult for me to see. I stopped on a telephone wire for a while till I felt better then yet again set off on my long journey.

When I was flying I met so many other swifts going to South America but they were babies, so they couldn't fly as fast as me, therefore they just lagged behind. After a few days I got to America and I liked it so much better than Scotland. It was much hotter and had lots more food. I also met another swift that I shared a tree with. He was very handsome and could fly much better than all the other birds. After a while we fell in love and I had 3 chicks, they were so gorgeous and we couldn't wait to teach them how to fly and the ways of the world.

A couple of weeks later they were ready to leave the nest so us parents flew out first and they followed. After crash-landing, which was really funny, they all soon got the hang of it. It soon came to the end of our stay in America and we were to fly back with the kids, but just as we were about to leave, one of the kids fell out of the nest. We soon got him back up to the nest but he couldn't fly. It was going to get cold soon so I told the kids to carry on and go back to Scotland with their dad and I would stay here and look after their brother.

During the cold and windy weather my son passed away from being so cold and then I fell ill and fell out of the nest. I knew I would die but it was for the best. I couldn't get food and was unable to look after myself, so I kissed my dead son goodbye and fell from the tree.

Emma Louise Mayhew (13)
Sherwood Hall School & Sixth Form College, Mansfield

Detective Story

It was a normal day for Bob, Bill, Gary, Luke, Mary, Jack and Jill. The seven teenagers had been let out early from school due to summer exams. They had decided to take the train into London to do some shopping. The train station was deserted. The one o'clock train had not arrived. Bob, Gary, Luke and Mary went to nick some sweets from the empty station shop. Jill went to find some toilets leaving Bill and Jack, who had never really got on, alone on the platform.

'Oi pea brain! Gimmie a sweet now!' yelled Bill.

'Get your own you little moron!' exclaimed Jack.

'Are you taking the micky out of my size again?' hollered Bill across the platform.

'N-n-no,' quivered Jack, beginning to sound scared. He took a step away from Bill but near the edge.

'Well it sounded like you were and I hate people talking about my size!' shouted Bill.

'L-l-look Bill, you know I wouldn't, we're mates right? Bill, Bill, what you doing, pal?' asked Jack, just as the train rounded the corner.

It all happened in seconds. Bill pushed Jack onto the tracks. Jill, just coming back from the toilets, saw her brother fall. She ran forward to grab him but missed. Bill, thinking fast, quickly advanced on Jill. He pushed her down onto the lline to meet her friend and brother. She screamed.

The train shot past Bill's face. He was now and for the rest of his life, a murderer. He looked down at the mangled bodies. Bob ran down the station, closely following were Gary, Luke and Mary.

'Dude, why didn't you stop the train?' Bob shouted, sounding confused.

'I-I-I ...' stuttered Bill.

'Spit it out mate!' Gary started to sound angry. 'It's hours till the next train!'

'Hey, where are Jack and Jill?' asked Mary, Jill's best friend.

Bill pointed down onto the line. The others looked down at the horrific sight. They gasped. Bill told them Jack and Jill had fought and fallen onto the tracks but he was too late to save them.

They rang the police and later that evening they found themselves sitting at Jack and Jill's parents' house, waiting to talk to the detective.

'Mrs White, Mr White, I know this is hard for you, you have been extremely helpful. Please ask the children to come in on your way out, thank you,' said Detective John-Jones.

'Good evening Detective,' chorused the teens.

'So … who was it that witnessed the incident?' asked the detective.

'It was me! It was all me! I'm so sorry, I didn't mean to do it!' shouted Bill. He ran out of the room and down the corridor to the balcony. He stopped for a minute, then, he jumped.

Case closed!

Heather Patton
Sherwood Hall School & Sixth Form College, Mansfield

A Day In The Life Of A Fish

I was swimming in the big blue (for you humans that's the sea) one morning when I realised that my life was actually good. It had never occured to me before now. I have a lovely husband, wonderful children and I live in the big blue which means I can swim all I like.

At the moment, I'm on my way to a coral. I love swimming throughout the fantastic aquamarine sea as the feel of the sea brushing up against my scales is amazing. I enjoy swimming with the current which is what I'm doing now.

What is that black shadow in the distance? It looks big and grey. It's approaching me quickly! No! It's a shark! Swim, swim, swim.

I'm hidden behind a rock. Please say the shark didn't see me. It's okay, the shark has gone. I hate sharks, they eat little fish like me all the time, they're so frightening.

Here I am, I'm at the coral. It is so pretty. The plants are pink and purple. It's fantastic. Every time I'm at the coral it is like being in Heaven. There are lots of fish happily swimming around me and the water is so still. You can watch bubbles rise up towards the sky.

All I do here is swim and swim. This place is so full of energy and life. However, sadly, it's time for me to go home now. Goodbye coral, I will be back soon.

Rachel Saunders
Sherwood Hall School & Sixth Form College, Mansfield

A Day In The Life Of A ...

It was an ordinary day in the drawer. I woke as usual ready for Bob to use me for his Coco Pops. Life didn't really get more interesting than that for a spoon. I might get to go outside if someone wants ice cream on the patio, but that would be all.

So there I was, in the drawer, when sure enough Bob slammed it open and grabbed me. I was the only spoon in that drawer. Bob lived by himself and didn't have many visitors.

I wasn't a bad-looking spoon in those days; brightly coloured, green plastic handle and a nice, shiny, stainless steel head. I was rather handsome.

Bob finished his Coco Pops and I got left on the draining board after a quick rinse. There I lay until, four hours later, Bob came home for lunch. It was strange - every meal he seemed to use me.

Today for lunch was last night's curry, cold, out of the fridge. Luckily I can't taste what I scoop, because it made Bob cry. Then, another rinse and I was back on the draining board for the afternoon. It wasn't so bad, being there for six hours; I had a really good conversation with Percy (one of the pegs) about the theory of relativity and I think I saw a pigeon. You don't normally see many pigeons as a spoon.

When Bob came home for his tea that evening, he had beans on toast. He always puts his beans in a bowl and has the toast separate, so a knife and fork were out of the question. He must have had a bad day because he had some rice pudding and he only has that when he needs cheering up. Bob ate his rice pudding in front of the telly, so I managed to catch bits of what was going on.

I slept in the bowl that night because Bob couldn't be bothered to tidy me up until the morning, which meant I got to watch 'Spider-Man' with him, which is always fun.

Although it can sometimes be a bit dull, I would never want to be anything other than a spoon.

Jenny Patten (14)
Sherwood Hall School & Sixth Form College, Mansfield

A Day In The Life Of A Cloud

Hello, I am a cloud and at the moment I am drifting over the ocean gathering rain to rain on someone.

I'm drifting towards Bob's house in Mansfield. I stopped and unleashed a torrent of rain. The rain lashed down onto his windows and house. The roof leaked and when I was empty I drifted once again towards the ocean, once again to gather rain.

On my way to the ocean I flew over the airport and a plane flew right through me. Ooooooh, that tickled.

After the encounter with the plane I carried on drifting towards the ocean to gather rain.

When I reached the ocean I stopped to gather some rain and then I saw a fisherman and decided to turn into a storm to make his life hell.

Ha, ha, ha, ha, ha, ha, that was really funny!

I was drifting over the Pacific ocean when a flock of geese flew through me. 'Ahhh! I'm breaking apart! Noooo!'

And that was the end of me.

Matthew Holt (14)
Sherwood Hall School & Sixth Form College, Mansfield

A Day In The Life Of A Pound Coin

I am sitting here in the bottom of Lizzie's purse surrounded by ten pence coins and twenty pence coins. I overheard Lizzie talking to her friends last night about going into town today so no doubt I will be going too. I can hear something moving around. Lizzie must be awake now.

I am now on Lizzie's bed. She is counting the rest of her money and me. She is putting all the money back in her purse; I am last to go in. We have now been put in her handbag. She is running downstairs and out the door shouting to her mum that she is going into town and will be back at around three.

It's about lunchtime now and I am back in Topshop's till. Lizzie bought a new top and used me to pay for it. Every five seconds there is another pound coin thrown in with the rest of us in this tiny little box. I just got chatting to another pound coin when it was taken away and put in an old woman's hand.

Still in Topshop except now I have moved tills. It must be about three o'clock now. There's a man with his daughter being served now. She has just made her dad buy her one hundred and ninety-nine pounds worth of clothes and I am going to be the pound change given. The dad is called John and I am now in his pocket along with his keys and other change.

John is now sat on a bar stool in a pub. Feeling around in his pocket I am given to the barman who drops me on the floor. I am kicked by a woman's stiletto heel under the bar. Here I will stay.

Victoria Winterton (13)
Sherwood Hall School & Sixth Form College, Mansfield

A Night You'd Never Want To Revisit!

Bolts of lightning flashed through the dark woods. The howl of wolves could be heard in the distance. The moon cast a glow upon the banks of the still river.

There was an awkward silence amongst the trees. A mysterious man stumbled through the mist. He had just been to the local and got lost on the way home. The man looked up to the trees and saw 5 pairs of red eyes staring back at him. They were owls. They flew straight into the man. He fell over and banged his head.

The man slowly opened his eyes and saw a lot of people standing around him. He was in Kings Mill Hospital. The doctor came round and told Mr Smith (the man) that he had been knocked unconscious and that his body could have failed him because he had too much alcohol in it. The doctor also said that he was very lucky to have been found by a woman walking her dog in the early hours of the morning.

The man recovered and every time that he goes to the local he is now only drinking pure orange juice.

Emma Whitten
Sherwood Hall School & Sixth Form College, Mansfield

A Shriek In The Night

Bolts of lightning flashed through the dark woods. The howl of a wolf could be heard in the distance. The moon cast a glow upon the crumbly ruins of Castle Dracula.

The eerie midnight silence was shattered by a sudden shriek that shook the birds from their nests. The noise of bare feet running on stone now echoed through the courtyard as a young woman in a flowing red dress ran in fear of her life. Her long brown hair distorted her vision as she quickened her pace. She didn't know who it was, she didn't know what it was, all she knew was that it gave her a feeling that made her blood run icy cold - and now it was chasing her.

'Sophia?' it called after her. 'You can't run forever.'

She glanced behind her as she fled in hope to see the creature, but only the darkness of the desolate hour glared back.

Darting her eyes forward once more, she ran towards the shelter of the woods in the endless wilderness, she continued until she was overcome with exhaustion, collapsed in a fragile heap of a broken soul. She was not yet dead but she could hear the shallow breath of the creature directly behind her. Although she fought with all her remaining power it effortlessly overpowered her, as she quietly cried for one last time.

Shana White
Sherwood Hall School & Sixth Form College, Mansfield

The Old Road Through The Woods

I walked through the ghostly wood. I was lost and didn't know what to do. There was a low hanging mist and a few drops of rain. The wind suddenly howled. The sound was like a million wolves howling together. I walked deeper and deeper into the woods until I couldn't see the road leading into the woods. The problem was there was no road through the woods. I heard an owl hoot loudly and something move in the leafy undergrowth.

Suddenly I heard a voice echo through the trees. I couldn't make out what it was saying because all of the birds moved quickly out of their treetop perches at the same time, making the sound almost disappear. Then I realised what had made all of the birds fly away. It was a horse that looked like a porcupine because of all the arrows sticking out of its body. Then my eyes were drawn to its rider. The rider had no head. In his hands he had two swords and they were being spun round like the blades of a helicopter. I couldn't work out what was happening until one of the swords hit me on the head. I fell to the floor. I was left on the floor where the old road used to be. Dead. I was dead!

Now I follow the headless rider to kill anyone who trespasses on our land …

Edward Swingler (11)
South Wigston High School, Wigston

A Day In The Life Of The Wishing Dragon

No one knows where he comes from,
No one knows where he goes.
No one knows of the wishes he makes,
But read on and you will know.

The wishing dragon is a very peculiar creature. He has two clawed feet covered in deep purple scales, large nostrils and ears like an elf. The odd thing about him though is he is human-sized!

He would disperse from his home in the clouds and search for food, usually finding a nice clump of grass or flowers from the field. Some children even found their sunflower heads nibbled off! They're a particular favourite! After he had eaten, he would search again, for a receiver ...

This is the person that the wish is granted for. They will say their wish while a ring of glittering smoke forms around their body. When they have done, a dainty twinkling sound surrounds them.

The dragon would choose a special child to spend the whole day with. The child would probably make some mischievous and fun wishes. Most of the time children decide to make themselves invisible and play fun tricks on their friends and family. They may even take an invisible ride on the dragon's back!

The day is nearly over for the little wishing dragon. Even though he has had fun he needs to rest for yet another adventure!

Everything has finished,
I've nothing else to say.
But what tomorrow brings,
Well, that's another day.

Katherine Ardley (11)
South Wigston High School, Wigston

Burn

Amanda could hear a crackling noise. She got out of bed and went to open the door. To her horror, as she opened the door, she could see thick black smoke. She quickly shut the door and rushed over to the window - panicking. There was obviously a fire, right there in her house.

Amanda breathed in the fresh air and tried to calm down. She suddenly shouted, *'Help!'* but nobody seemed to respond. She gave another cry of help. *'Help! Please help ... there's a fire in my house!'* She paused and coughed. She needed to hurry and call the fire brigade. The nearest phone was in the next room.

She bravely opened the door and started making her way to the next room. The fire had occurred in the guest bedroom, spreading towards the landing. Amanda edged away from the flames: she could really feel the heat. She plucked up the courage and darted into the computer room. She had made it. Grabbing the phone, Amanda dialled 999.

'Fire brigade, how may I help you?'

'There's a fire in my house,' spoke Amanda into the receiver. 'I live at 16 Blakewell Road.'

'We're on our way.'

Amanda put the phone down.

Within a few minutes, Amanda heard the sirens of the fire engine. The next moment the door was forced open.

'I'm up here!' called Amanda.

A fireman was extinguishing flames in his path. Amanda came out of the house. It was a heart-wrenching moment watching her house being destroyed.

Jessica Russell (11)
South Wigston High School, Wigston

You Only Live Once

'Ruth! Wake up girl, we haven't got all day,' yelled a vicious voice.

Ruth, a young kitchen maid, awoke to the head cook, a portly woman with greasy hair, blackened teeth and a foul smell that she carried everywhere.

'Yes Miss,' Ruth answered nervously, as Cook slammed the door behind her. Ruth was all alone in her cold, dark room.

Just a year ago she was with her loving family without a care in the world. Then, war broke out and her father was called up for service. Not long after, her father went missing in action and Ruth was sent to work in a manor house to earn the family money.

Later that day, as she was hanging out the washing, she cried with the pain from her sore hands. Through the tears she saw a familiar-looking figure in the distance, she was not sure who it was. She quickly dried her eyes and edged towards them. From that point the figure became a lot clearer. She forgot about the pain in her hands and ran towards him, her heart beating like a drum ...

'Ruth, Ruth,' whispered a soft, calming voice. Doctor Watson gently brought Ruth out of her hypnosis.

They discussed Ruth's experience about her supposed past life.

'I think next time we will try to find out more about this figure,' suggested Doctor Watson.

As Ruth left the office, she remembered a saying she had heard. 'You only live once', and she smiled as she left the building.

Rebecca Hemsley (11)
South Wigston High School, Wigston

Timber!

As James walked through the woods at the back of his house he heard an unfamiliar sound. At first he couldn't work out what it was but as he drew closer, he could make out the sound of a man's voice and a chainsaw. As he drew even closer, he could hear the man's voice crying, 'Timber!'

All the birds flew out of the trees and there was a humongous crash and there before him lay a giant tree.

Then, before he knew it, the trees around him began shrinking and women in white pinafores came hurrying through, totally oblivious of him.

He walked rapidly after them to somewhere where he vaguely recognised. Then it clicked. In his history lessons (which he'd hardly been paying attention in) he'd learnt about the Victorians. This was his town in the Victorian ages.

He now knew he had to get back. His town couldn't carry on living in the Victorian ages whilst all the rest of the world were up to date with medicines and all the new technology. He had to get back, but how? He began to panic.

Then he felt his sweaty bedsheets and opened his bleary eyes just in time to hear the word, 'Timber!'

Charlotte Button (11)
South Wigston High School, Wigston

Harry Potter And The Prisoner Of Azkaban's Script
(Based on 'Harry Potter and the Prisoner of Azkaban' by J K Rowling)

Scene 1: Dursley's Home (morning)

Harry: (coming down the stairs as phone rings)

Uncle Vernon: (comes into the hall, picks up the phone) 'Vernon Dursley speaking.'

Ron Weasley: (Ron bellows down the phone) 'Hello? Hello! Can you hear me? I-want-to-talk-to-Harry-Potter!'

Uncle Vernon: (screaming down the phone) 'Who is this? Who are you?'

Ron Weasley: (shouting) 'Ron-Weasley-I'm-a friend-from-Hogwa-...'

Uncle Vernon: (roaring) 'I don't know any Harry Potter, I don't know what school you're on about, don't you dare ever come near my family, you hear!' (slams the phone down) 'You.' (pointing at Harry) 'How dare you give this number to people like ... people like ... you.'

Harry: 'You never said I couldn't and anyway you might not know this but I'm older than Dudley because at 12.00 this morning I turned 13 but you don't care do you? No!'

Uncle Vernon: 'How dare you speak to me in that ungrateful tone? Why you're standing there in clothes your aunt and I put you in.'

Harry: 'Only when Dudley had finished with them! I'm going out for some fresh air, it's better than spending my birthday here with you lot. (walks to the door, opens it, about to step outside)

Uncle Vernon: 'Don't be too long; I want you to look nice for Aunt Marge.'

Harry: (turns around quickly) 'Aunt Marge isn't coming is she?'

Uncle Vernon: 'Yes, and she doesn't know about your school and we will keep it that way, right?'

Harry: 'Alright, but only if you sign my form.'

Uncle Vernon: 'Only if you behave until Marge has gone.'

Harry: 'Right, OK, deal.'

Rebecca Norton (11)
South Wigston High School, Wigston

Back In Time

'Hurry up!' shouted Mum to Hannah and Thomas. 'We haven't got all day.'

Mum, Hannah and Thomas were cleaning out Grandad's attic after he had died.

'These boxes are heavy,' exclaimed Hannah.

'My arms are dropping off,' moaned Thomas.

Hannah and Thomas dropped the boxes on the attic floor. Mum went to get more boxes.

'What's that?' asked Thomas, pointing and running towards a box.

A glow appeared and filled the room.

'It's some kind of light source,' replied Hannah.

Before she could say any more, a clatter of light swept them into the air, whirling round and round.

Suddenly they were lowered to the ground with a thump. They had not yet realised that they had left the attic and were now sitting in a shelter.

'What was that?' asked Thomas, rubbing his bottom.

'I'm not sure,' said Hannah. 'Some kind of light made us travel.'

'W-w-where are w-w-we?' stuttered Thomas.

'I think we have travelled back in time to World War II!' exclaimed Hannah.

'I'm getting out of here,' cried Thomas, rushing for the exit of the shelter.

'No!' shouted Hannah. 'It could be dangerous.'

It was too late. Thomas was standing in the middle of a bombing. He looked above. Speeding towards him was a bomb which was going to bomb the house he was standing next to.

Another flash of light appeared. The next minute Hannah and Thomas were safely back in their grandad's attic.

'Thank God that's over,' puffed Thomas in relief.

Alice Dale (11)
South Wigston High School, Wigston

Revenge Or Die!

Alex Jones awoke in a hospital bed, feeling nauseous. He could clearly remember the sound of gunshots, and the sight of his parents' bloodstained bodies lying on the grimy footpath beside him, their wounds were fatal. Alex could vaguely remember the Hummer H2 speeding away before he slipped into unconsciousness.

Grimacing, he slowly climbed out of bed and got dressed, determined to extract his revenge on the people who had murdered his parents. Alex slowly limped down the crowded streets. He knew who had killed his parents. They were part of a ruthless street gang who loitered around in the abandoned warehouse downtown. Alex felt a flood of hatred for the men overwhelm him. He was determined to track them down and kill them for all the grief they had caused him.

On arrival at the warehouse, Alex quickly scanned the area for any guards. Seeing one, Alex picked up one of the many iron bars from the floor and sneaked up behind the guard. Alex swung the bar as hard as he could at the man's head, killing him instantly. He glanced down at the figure lying in the pool of blood, and briefly removed the man's sawn-off shotgun and 12-inch knife.

Unfortunately, Alex had not noticed the sniper crouching on the warehouse rooftops. Alex had no chance when the Teflon-coated bullet hit him just below the heart. Alex had failed his mission and this time there were no paramedics at hand to rescue him ...

Daniel Bell (13)
Springwell Community School, Chesterfield

The Demonic Proposition

Kerry laid there sleeping, but still she was restless. There was something on her mind, probably the recent visits she had been having from a ghost, yes, a poltergeist. The cause of her fretful nights.

She woke early the next morning, only to be greeted by her new found friend. The friend without a name, who had quite literally been haunting her.

'Been thinking about my offer?'

Just the sentence she had been hoping not to hear. She had barely opened her eyes only to be greeted by the presence of an apparition. The spirit had been watching her through the night. Creepy to think of somebody watching you sleep. Waiting for the answer he was looking for.

He had offered her an opportunity to have the life she had longed for, a life with her mother. A life which she thought would never exist.

One of the most desolating days a child could have to go through, on her eighth birthday. Just as they sat down to eat their meal, the phone rang. Her mother answered and received the news she didn't want to hear. The devastating news that after her recent tests, her cancer had spread and she had less than six months to live. She managed to hold back the tears at dinner, but broke down afterwards and told Kerry the facts.

The sleepless nights started then, she would never be the same. Her thirteenth birthday had just gone and all the memories had come rushing back.

She had been thinking about the ghost's offer. Should she accept? It was a serious decision which would affect the rest of her life and rewrite history. But to have her dreams as reality would be truly phenomenal.

The slow day passed, her very thoughts diminishing and her mind focusing on the one decision she had to make. Should she bring her mother back? The more she thought about it, the more tempting the idea seemed. She loved her mother more than anything and even one more day with her would fulfil her deepest wishes.

That night she lay in her lonely bed, thinking back to the days when she would lay there with her mother as she was scared of the dark. Her mother would comfort her and wash all her fears away. Her thoughts were distracted by the demonic voice once again.

'Have you come to a decision? I know you have been thinking about my proposition very carefully, but I need an answer now!' bellowed the phantom.

Kerry had come to a decision. 'Yes, I want the life I hardly had, a life with my mother.'

Her words echoed and a fetid smell arose, her vision blurred then ... she saw her mother emerge from the darkness into the light. She was euphoric but still something seemed wrong. It was surreal. Kerry tried to speak but she could not find the words. She was overwhelmed but as she looked over her mother's shoulder, she saw her very own lifeless body, motionless on her bed. What could she say? She had been played for a fool, her own life had been taken away!

'Good choice, young girl, you've got what you longed for, a life with your mother and I've got what I wanted, to be human again!'

Kerry grimaced with a feeling of trepidation but the comforting sound of her mother's voice took all her pain away.

'There is no need to be scared of the dark now Kerry, you'll always be in the everlasting light with me.'

Siobhan Kelly (12)
Springwell Community School, Chesterfield

Granted!

In the minuscule village of Down Under, at the bottom of the ocean, lived a young mermaid named Christall. She was only 14 years of age and thought the world revolved around her. She always took her father for granted. Well, that was until the magic sea horse came along.

Late one seaday afternoon, Christall's father asked to see her.

'Y-y-yes Father,' she stammered, as she knew exactly what he was going to say to her. It was the same old lecture she got every day.

'Christall,' said her father, glaring at her with a raised eyebrow, 'I am sick of you acting like such a deranged child and taking me for granted, expecting me to give you money how and when you want it. It stops now, Christall!'

Christall swam up to her room in rage. 'That's it,' she said to herself as she punched her pillow.

Later that night, Christall swam off, not knowing where she was going to end up. After a couple of hours of swimming she decided to lay down for a nap. She tried her hardest to get to sleep but it was no use. She was lost, cold and tired and she started to realise how she shouldn't take her father for granted. As she was just about to fall to sleep, something caught her eye. It was the magic sea horse.

'I promise I will take you home if you promise me you'll not take anyone for granted.'

Christall agreed and their promises were granted!

Abbi Carter (13)
Springwell Community School, Chesterfield

Trapped On Mars

One day, in the life of Lucia and Tara, their daily routine was about to turn very strange. Nobody knows why it happened.

Lucia and Tara were strolling down the narrow pathways of Rome when they both stopped. Their worst enemy was stood right in front of them but for some reason she was being very benevolent.

'Hi Jade, are you feeling OK today?' asked Tara.

'I'm fine, now get out of my way, I need to get out of here *quickly!*' yelled Jade.

Why did she need to leave so quickly? thought Lucia. They were worried. Then *bang!* A massive cloud of smoke filled the street. Then Lucia looked round to talk to Tara but there was no Tara.

What planet's this? wondered Tara. It didn't look like Earth at all. It was bright red and was boiling. It couldn't be Mars, it was full of humans and it was said that humans would burn if they lived on Mars. She must have gone into the future.

A message showed on the wall. It read, 'Your friend will be back once you do what we want you to do'.

'I'll do it!' Lucia yelled.

'Go into the school library and get us the books on teenage life.'

She did so, then returned with them. They said she had to wait for a while so they could check they were right. Then they said that they would bring Tara back.

What's going on? I can't move, thought Tara ...

Gemma Beach (13)
Springwell Community School, Chesterfield

The Lost Prince

The princess sat at the side of her grandad's grave, just talking about how she needed him to help her and what she needed to do to get back the prince she loved. She started to cry.

Suddenly she felt a breeze across the back of her neck and goosebumps from head to toe. A voice spoke.

'Here my dear child, I will help you.'

She knew it was her grandad. The princess told him everything that had happened. How she'd met a prince and fallen madly in love, then how he'd broken her heart as he'd found someone else to love, but how he still always spoke to her and she'd go all funny and get butterflies.

Her grandad simply spoke the words, 'My dear, I can only say you just have to tell him how you feel, your true feelings, don't lie.'

'Thank you Grandad, thank you, I love you.' She ran to find her prince.

On her way she bumped into him.

The prince said, 'Are you OK?'

She softly said, 'I love you.' Then she told him everything she felt and how he'd hurt her.

He just said he was very sorry for everything he had done but ... he was leaving and he was never coming back. She started to cry and watched as he got into a car and they said their goodbyes. They were both crying as he drove away. Their lives, hearts and souls ripped apart. Never to see each other again ...

Skye Hopkinson (13)
Springwell Community School, Chesterfield

Cherry Bomb

I click my seatbelt off and pull myself out of the wreck that was once a spotless cherry-red Fiat. The windscreen smashed into a million shards of glass, each with a piece of trapped sunlight glittering in the late noon light.

In the front seat my parents are slumped over the dashboard, their tongues almost comically lolling, faces bruised and bleeding. I run and wrestle with the passenger door and wish it to open. I rush in and pull my mum and dad out of the car and onto the soft grass. My tears overwhelm me and finally break the barrier I've made. No one needs to tell me. I already know they're gone.

The front door clicks shut and I run to my parents' room to find something that shows that they were here, alive, in this very house with me as their daughter. I smell the room - Mum's clothes still smell of the musky perfume she loved and Dad's left his curly hair in the plug again.

I lay on the bed and in the kitchen a tap is turned on. I'm alone. I run and turn it off. Then my mum and dad appear before me and tell me to go to the apple tree in the garden. I run with them floating behind to the tree. The tree is glittering with stars, but as I look closer they are really fairies.

All in a swoosh I feel happy and relaxed and the fairies are wiping all my troubles away. Then it goes black ...

Rebecca Bateman (13)
Springwell Community School, Chesterfield

The Well Of Dreams

This place was not normal. It was like she had travelled to another world. It was so quiet and harmonious. No traffic, pollution, not even any sign of life! It was surreal. Then she noticed a narrow opening in the bark of a tree. She went to take a closer look. 'Ow,' she screeched. Something had bit her on the nose. She looked again. 'Ow.' There it was again. She put in her hand, grabbed at something and pulled out what looked like a ... no, it couldn't be ... yes it was, a ... *fairy!*

She had read about these in books but she didn't think they were real. There was something not right about the look of this fairy. She looked like her little sister did when she had the mumps a few years ago, but much worse. The fairy started to cry.

'Why are you sad?' she asked.

'I have an illness called Blazing Fever and all that can cure it is a drink from the well of dreams at the end of a gruelling obstacle course!' the fairy replied.

She dropped the fairy and ran as fast as she could. She stopped. In front of her was a large door. She ventured through it and she did not expect what it was hiding. Through the door was an obstacle course, but not any ordinary obstacle course. This course led up to the well of dreams. It looked dangerous. That's when she made her first fatal mistake. She stood on the wrong stepping stone ... !

Natalie Lee (12)
Springwell Community School, Chesterfield

A Day In The Life Of Gulch The Gnome

If you saw me on a typical gnome car boot sale you wouldn't know what I have been through. If I told you, I would be breaking all the gnome rules, plus you would tell another mudgiant, but here goes ...

I was relaxing, you know, sitting on a stone, rod in my hand, catching plastic fish. Yeah, I wish, what I really was doing was travelling 3,000 miles underground. Well what do you think we do all day? Just sit around when there's saving the mudgiants to do?

Well, don't look at me like that. We gnomes may be small, but we do save the human race a lot. I remember my first mission in 1966, I had to detonate the lobster foot (biobomb). It did go smoothly, until we met that schwat of a fairy (if I translated schwat it would be no good).

That fairy only set the biobomb off and killed every mudgiant within 100ft.

I bet if you saw me now you'd know me. As interesting as I am you would want to know me, wouldn't you? Just think, could you handle me?

Kelsey Stirling (13)
Springwell Community School, Chesterfield

The Life Of A Spoilt Child

Let me introduce myself to you. I'm Louise Nicholson and my daddy owns the largest company in the whole of the UK!

Well, back to my story, it was just like any other day, I woke up and Prudence (our maid) brought me my breakfast. *Crash!* Well, what was left of it, anyway. I got dressed in my new playing out clothes - a Gucci dress. I went downstairs and told my daddy about what had happened.

'Daddy, Prudence dropped my breakfast again! Why can't we get a new maid?'

'Because darling, you go through 8 maids a month and you've only had Prudence 3 days.'

'Yes and every one of those 3 days that dumb idiot has dropped my breakfast.'

'Well, let's give her a few more days.'

'OK.'

I was a little disappointed that he hadn't fired her. It was the first time I had been told no in 9 years and I'm only 10! Then I went out to play in the garden. Suddenly, out of nowhere, this tiny creature flew towards me. I was mesmerised. The creature was very beautiful - long, flowing hair, tiny silver wings and dainty features.

'I am Alana, queen of the fairies. Now I've heard that you are very spoilt and we're going to stop that! Oh small child, spoilt and rotten, you will be good or get a smacked bottom!'

With that she was gone and from that day on I've been good!

Jade Davies (13)
Springwell Community School, Chesterfield

Up, Over And Wet

Sammy stood beside her pony, Apollo. Sammy was next to go into the show jumping ring. The jumps looked high and Sammy felt nervous. No one had yet got a clear round.

Apollo's mane and tail were all plaited up for the occasion and Sammy stood wearing her show outfit.

The bell rang for Sammy to enter the ring. She started to trot around the ring with Apollo doing what he was asked. Sammy cantered up to the first jump and cleared it easily. The next two jumps were placed in a double so Apollo found it harder to get his stride right. Apollo knocked one jump but luckily it just wobbled and didn't fall. There were 10 jumps altogether and Sammy was on her seventh and was clear up to now. Apollo was starting to get excited so he wasn't taking much care in what he was doing. He was getting faster by the minute and jumping very long over the poles. The water jump was coming up and Sammy knew that she had to get Apollo under control to be able to clear it.

Apollo started to race towards the water jump. All of a sudden, Apollo stopped and refused to jump, throwing Sammy out of the saddle, over the poles and into the water. Sammy sat up in the water. Unhurt, she looked around at the crowd and laughed and laughed. It had been an eventful day!

Heather Thomas (13)
Springwell Community School, Chesterfield

South Pole Patrol

How can I describe Professor Plank? He's a delirious world observer. Despite the fact that he passed college with faultless grades, he was shut up in a decrepit castle on an outrageously high hill and, because of old age, he had unfortunately lost his marbles. To prove this, his current observation was to find out how penguins were trying to save the world from destruction. (He may not have been as bonkers as first thought.) He managed to spy on the penguins through a secret camera system set up in the South Pole.

Plank had studied the amount of pollutants going up into the ozone layer and as far as he could tell, the world would not end for 1,059 years yet. But the penguins were 100 years ahead of them in technology and it was the year 4126.

Meanwhile, down in the South Pole, the penguin police were waiting for a computer to tell them how long they had to save the world. The computer grunted and groaned.

'Hurry up you blasted thing,' shouted Chief Waddle, red-faced.

Obediently the printer spat out a piece of paper stating 23,942,693 hours!

'What the ... ?' exclaimed the headquarters' manager.

'We need longer!' raged Waddle (plum now).

'Get moving then,' ordered the HQ manager.

'Sid, Jeremy, you're on lookout. Any humans set off the alarm, the rest of you in your planes and destroy; cars, lorries, powerstations, everything that pollutes the air,' demanded Waddle.

The headquarters' manager had set up a counting system on the computer with every type of powerstation or polluter - how many still in tact and how many destroyed by the penguin police.

Professor Plank turned on his secret camera system only to find a deserted police office. *Bang!* The power went off.

'They're up to something,' he mumbled to himself.

'W-w-we only have 10 minutes,' stammered Waddle. 'We're not going to make it!'

The headquarters' manager was now panicking. 2,346 pollutants left, 56 officers, 5 minutes to go. 250 pollutants, 56 officers, 1 minute, 30 seconds, 10, 9, 8, 7, 6, 5, 4, 3, 2, 1, *flash, bang, rumble!* ...

Kerry McPhail (13)
Springwell Community School, Chesterfield

The Secret Hand

'It's too loud in here, I'm going to look for a taxi,' shouted Faith.

No one seemed to have heard her. She took a look back, hoping that somebody would go with her, but everyone was having too much fun.

She stormed out, looking at the bouncers with a very evil eye. Her hand was in and out, in and out, trying to stop a taxi, but none of them did.

'Hey, I didn't know you were out tonight,' said Faith.

'Yes, well, I felt a little less euphoria.'

Faith walked off with a very big smile on her face, knowing that she had seen her sister. Then suddenly out of nowhere, this hand grabbed hold of her and pulled her into an alleyway.

'Argh, get off me, please don't hurt me,' Faith shouted at the top of her voice.

The man's hand went straight over Faith's mouth with all the sweat of his hand. Faith tried to keep her mouth shut. He started feeling her in places where she felt uncomfortable. She knew he was going to rape her, she just knew it. He started to unbutton her top, then her short, tight miniskirt. He pulled it straight down.

'Get off me, please.' She struggled and struggled but he was too strong. She didn't know what to do, she tried to knee him but he was too close and too tight on her.

He was getting closer and closer then there was a voice.

'Step away from her or somebody is going to get hurt ...'

Leigh-Marie Swan (13)
Springwell Community School, Chesterfield

The War Of All Time

'Take cover,' bellowed Master Commando Steve.

Speeding bullets flew overhead whilst they were moving furtively towards their underground base. The army force (AFO) were not so far behind.

Commando Mark was already in the base, using top of the range software trying to figure out the locations of the robots. 'We need to make a plan and we need to make a plan quickly, they are heading this way. Right, here it is, we'll send in the army force out as the front line and us two will get in a tank each, *right!*'

The army force crept slowly out of the hatch, trying not to get caught. Steve and Mark ran to a tank each, both climbed inside one and started the engines. The tank Mark was in had deep red bloodstains up all the walls from the commando who went out before him. Luckily the AFO had managed to retrieve it from the battleground.

They went up the ramp in the tanks and were creeping behind the AFO. They stood their ground for a short time. They couldn't see the robots for a while and then there they were appearing from the distance. '3 … 2 … 1 … *fire!*' Steve and Mark fired the fierce bullets right towards them, the bombs landing just in front, just as they wanted. The AFO were shooting all their bullets towards the robots but the robots didn't seem to be dying; they just kept on moving towards the troops.

Mark saw this huge round boulder coming straight for his tank …

Jamie Barnett
Springwell Community School, Chesterfield

A Day In The Life Of A Hired Murderer

I got up this morning feeling terrible. The night before I was involved in a shooting, I killed the guy I was meant to but I also killed his toddler. I don't enjoy my job. The killing isn't hard. It's hard making sure I haven't left evidence for the police. I am in the hired thug business, it is a dangerous career.

I checked my agenda, three middle-aged men to kill today. I only kill men, never women; I suppose I am sexist. The men had been feeding the police information on my boss, with his 'dealings'. If there is one thing I hate, it is squealers.

I loaded my gun and went to the address of the first man. I drove up to his stately manor. I trudged up to his door, looking at the grey misty clouds, they floated so freely. I knocked on the door twice. The door swung open violently, six police officers pinned me to the ground, one was standing up with his wavy brown hair, he was the sort of man I wish I could be, a hero, not a villain. The police were attacking me like lions shredding an antelope in the African savannah. If I had just been more careful I would not be in this jail cell.

Sometimes I wish I had children, but there is no point having loved ones in a job where you can get locked up at any time. I always choose the dangerous path, that's how I get by.

Mariam Ahmed (13)
The Garendon High School, Loughborough

Are You Home Before Dark?

'Come on, Mel! Mum said I have to be home before dark!' Izzy, her golden hair glinting in the sunset, was becoming a little scared. There had been an escaped convict in the next town that had murdered two girls just last week!

'One last kick around. Please!' Mel pleaded, her slim figure a shadow against the goal.

'OK, 3 shots each. I'll go in goal first.' Izzy was walking over to the goal when she noticed a shadowy figure approaching Mel. 'Mel, I think we should go now!' Izzy's voice was shaking and she felt her body go cold with fear. *'Mel! Mel!'*

'What now?'

But it was too late; when Mel turned round to take the shot, the shadowy figure grabbed her and started running with her. Izzy let out a shrill, high-pitched scream and tried to catch up; but when she did he smacked her round the face and left her lying on the grass. Izzy couldn't get up, but she had her mobile in her pocket so she dialled 999. An ambulance came to pick her up and took her straight to the hospital.

Izzy had a broken leg from the way she had landed, but there was no sign of Mel or the escaped convict, Jeff Lote. For the next week they heard nothing, there were no signs or clues to where she was; but then 2 weeks later the police found the body of Melanie Hethy in a wheelie bin outside 47 Patford Close.

Helen Orr (13)
The Garendon High School, Loughborough

The Minotaur

An uncertain eerie mist hung in the air which twirled and coiled through the desolate tunnel. Turning hastily on her heel, she studied the end of the tunnel carefully for she thought she could hear a noise, one which was not familiar to her. It was a steady rasping sound, which could only be that of the breath of another living creature, the Minotaur. Grabbing the rigid wall with her delicate fingers she gripped it tightly to keep her balance and guided herself along the damp tunnel trying to escape the noise of the unsightly creature, but gradually the originally soft breathing grew louder and louder until she felt the warm, stale smell of rotting flesh on the back of her neck.

Tensing the bottom of her stomach, she forced a scream which rolled up her throat and penetrated the once calm air into a frenzy of soundwaves, bouncing off walls and sending an echo rumbling down endless tunnels. The Minotaur grabbed her wrist and held it between his claw-like fingers, gripping with such almighty strength that she knew her skin would be left with painful grooves. He pulled her round swiftly to face him, licking his tender lips with his lizard-like tongue, whilst she squirmed desperately to break the burly grip on her wrist, with not much success. He opened his mouth, revealing a set of sharp, bloodstained teeth and gradually lowered his mouth onto her slim and delicate neck …

Hannah Bailey (13)
The Garendon High School, Loughborough

Missing In The Snow

Wrapped up in many layers, Madam Cornbekk hastened along the platform to catch her train. Just as the whistle blew, she was seeing the Wagon Lit conductor about her berth on the train. Another person's luggage had been placed there.

'Pardon Madam, it was a silly mistake. I will see to it personally.'

'You should be more careful in future, who knows what might happen? I heard that an American lady had been robbed and murdered on a train. Funny how this Belgian detective could work it all out. I do ho-'

'That would be Hercule Poirot, famous for solving complex murders as in that very case.'

The man who had just spoken was small with an egg-shaped head and black moustache. During the intrusion, the conductor had gone to sort Madam Cornbekk's luggage and berth. As Madam was curious and also disliked the interruption, she asked the name of the speaker.

'Why, I am M Poirot! Eh bien, I assure you that no harm shall come to any aboard such as yourself. Après vous Madam.'

So with a curt bow, M Poirot went to the dining car and Madam Cornbekk retired to her berth.

It was snowing heavily outside and the motion of the train was slow and uneven. After many attempts of trying to sleep, Madam Cornbekk arose from her bed and walked into the corridor. The cold air took her by surprise. Almost instantly, she realised something was seriously wrong … !

Rachel Blanchard (12)
The Garendon High School, Loughborough

A Day In The Life Of Laura Campbell

Laura Campbell won a bronze medal for the 4x100m medley relay in which she did the butterfly leg at the European Junior Championships 2003. Here is an account of what a day in her life might consist of.

Yesterday I got up at 4am as usual. I had a bowl of cereal before leaving for training at Handsworth pool in Birmingham at 4.10. Along the way I went to collect some of my friends and gave them a lift to be ready for training which starts at 5am.

Tiring though it may be I do this every day and in a typical two hour session my friends and I will do about 3,000 metres or more. Training finishes at 7am and I have to go back to Stourbridge where I live for half an hour to get ready for college and have something to eat. College starts at 8.45am and as I had a free lesson first I went back to bed for a bit because I was a little tired after getting up so early.

College finishes at 3.30pm and I went home straight away to collect my swimming kit and get back into Birmingham for the evening training session from 4.15 until 6.15. Training was fairly difficult last night because we were set twenty lots of a hundred metres and had to do each hundred within ten seconds of our personal best for that particular stroke. After that I did an hour of land training before going home for tea and to do my homework before going to bed at roughly half-past nine for another early start the next day.

Rachel Thorpe (13)
The Garendon High School, Loughborough

A Day In The Life Of A Dog

At 6 o'clock the alarm goes off and my day begins. My owner gets ready for work and I get to go outside!

When my owner is leaving for work I get into my harness and hop into the backseat of the car, looking out of the window. When my owner is working there is not much to do. I find a toy to play with and do all I can to enjoy myself.

When it is time to go back home my harness goes back on and I get back into the car. When I get back home I get let out of my harness and it is time for dinner! My preferred flavour is beef but I like any flavour.

In the evening I can do what I like as long as I don't get into trouble! After a long day I start to feel tired and try to get to sleep on the floor, but I prefer my kennel, so I go outside and get into it. Finally I get to sleep.

James Fairminer (13)
The Garendon High School, Loughborough

Civilisation ...

'It's too late!' cried the general, plunging his sword into the fertile soil. A vast storm cloud spread across the land and flames rose with menacing haste, surrounding the general's armies. 'We are too weak,' he moaned. 'The entire planet has been overrun!' His last word was muffled out as strange, incendiary devices poured from the sky like a savage rainstorm, destroying all in their path. One struck the general and he immediately fell to the floor, trying to put out the fires that had shrouded him. His struggling ended just a few seconds later as the burns took over his body. He was dead. A few nearby soldiers cried out loud and launched rockets into the sky to try and shake the enemy's war ships, who continued to fire down to Earth.

The atmosphere was immense. Shrill, demented choirs of wailing shells shattered the rocks and human bones that were lying around the battlefield, burned and broken. The world had come to a dramatic climax. Thousands of helpless soldiers stood firing into the sky, but to no avail. The cloud had prevented everyone from seeing the enemy looming over them, setting fire to all the land.

'I never thought civilisation would end this way,' exclaimed a soldier with a dull look on his face.

'Look!' another yelled.

Only those nearby could hear his words. He was pointing to a blue light coming down in the distance. Although it was far away, they could see it shining brightly on the horizon. They looked uncertain. The light disappeared out of sight and moments later they heard a faint rumbling noise.

Suddenly they all realised what had happened and they all looked into the distance. A huge wave was coming to them at a frightening pace. Some of them screamed and some just stood there, their eyes wide with horror. It was coming, coming, coming ...

Edward Burdett (13)
The Garendon High School, Loughborough

The Monster

In the cave, the monster stood. It stood still, waiting for its prey. The monster, who was feared by everybody, breathed heavily. Along the road was a small boy. Strolling along the pavement, the boy whistled to himself. Within seconds the boy was captured and was dead.

The monster had killed hundreds of people, girls, boys, children and adults - he had murdered them all. Everybody knew who he was and how dangerous he was, so why didn't anybody do anything to him? Nobody dared. That was until one day when two brave children dared to challenge the monster.

Their names were Jack and Maria. They were brother and sister. On one dark and spooky night they went towards the cave of the monster. The monster had heard the children and went to the edge of his cave. He saw Jack and Maria and got ready to attack. Cold and frightened, Maria ran at the monster. The monster, who did not expect this, did not have time to jump at Maria. Maria drew a knife from her pocket and stabbed the monster to death.

A few days later, Jack and Maria went back to the cave where the monster used to live. They explored the cave and found nothing in it except one thing - another monster. It was the monster's little brother. As soon as the new monster saw Jack and Maria he gobbled them up.

So a monster still stood in the cave that killed everybody that came near it.

Steven Bajor (13)
The Garendon High School, Loughborough

The Polish Resistance

'Watch out Sam. As soon as you hit that door the enemy will be on us. They are buzzing around the outside of our base like a beehive full of bees. They are also armed. We need you to sprint through that gang of German soldiers like an Olympic athlete. We will be with you all the way.'

Just as Sam touched the door, the German soldiers were firing at him with their rifles. He took a wound to the leg.

'Come on Sam!' I screamed as I picked him up, still trying to avoid enemy fire.

Bang! Bang! Bang! The gunshots were flying in from all angles, like eagles chasing their prey. Only one thing kept us going, the thought of freedom for ourselves and fellow countrymen.

Finally we saw off enemy fire and the German base was in sight.

'I can't carry on,' said Sam. 'Leave me here.'

I refused to do so. We sneaked up to the enemy base and began putting gun holes in the German base door.

They easily shrugged off our fire though but we kept battling for our country's safety. Suddenly grenades were blowing up all around us! I saw my friend's dead body lying around. I was alone.

I kept fighting until the end was coming fast. 'No!' I screamed as an enemy grenade stuck to my back. Is this the end for me and Poland?

Neil Taylor (12)
The Garendon High School, Loughborough

A Day In The Life Of A Cat

I got out of my snugly rug just after the sun had risen over the large tall trees. As I looked I saw that my bowl had been refilled the night before and so had my water bowl. I ate a little bit, I would save the rest until later. I lapped up a little water, then I went out the flap. Looking around the garden, I saw the damp grass shining in the morning sun. On the concrete slabs there was my dead mouse from the other night. I gnawed at it for a few seconds. Then, at the sound of a loud bang from one of the human's big metal machines, I sprinted to the fence and jumped up. Keeping a good balance I walked along at the top of the fence and jumped down into the front garden. Then, looking around, my yellow eyes caught sight of next-door's cat. I jumped at it but yet again it escaped me. All that day I tried to find him but without success.

When my owner returned I sprinted inside after her and finished off the beautifully tasty food bowl. I went into the big room to see that the big black screen had been turned on. I sat down in front of it and, even though it makes no sense to me, I sat there perfectly still for hours. Then she turned it off, scratched behind my ears and went upstairs. I returned to my rug and settled after a tiring day.

Andrew Robinson (13)
The Garendon High School, Loughborough

Hercules And The Lernaen Hydra

The Second Task Of Hercules: Destroy The Lernaen Hydra

The next opponent was the many-headed monster called the Hydra. Some said it had three heads and some said it had nine. No one could agree on exactly how many heads it really had. Its breath was so deadly that even the smell of its footprint was enough to kill any mortal being, but Hercules, being half god, did not die.

Hercules tracked down and found the monster and attempted to cut off one of its heads, only to find that two more sprouted back in place of the one he had just cut off. The long, snake-like heads then coiled themselves around his body.

He then remembered his nephew, Iolaus, who had driven him to the place of the Hydra. At first his nephew tried not to pay attention to his uncle's cries, but eventually gave up and ran to help. They then became a team. While Hercules cut the head, Iolaus scorched the wounds before more heads grew back.

When there was only one head left, which was supposedly immortal, Hercules trapped the monster inside a cave and barricaded it with a boulder.

Ethan Barnes (12)
The Garendon High School, Loughborough

The Missing ...

Aimee felt a hand tenderly brush away a tear that was slowly trickling down her cheek.

'Don't cry Aimee,' were the words whispered into her ear by a soft, placid voice, 'he'll be back soon.'

Aimee slowly turned to face the speaker. It was Darren. Darren was Aimee's next-door neighbour and they knew each other more like brother and sister than just friends. Like Aimee, Darren was thirteen years old, but tall for his age, with thick black hair, green eyes and ordinarily-shaped features. Aimee's mother thought that he was a very handsome young man. Nevertheless Aimee thought that he seemed to wear the same clothes every day, but still, he was her friend and she thanked him for that.

'How can you be so sure?' she replied. 'How do you know that he'll ever come back?'

'Of course he'll come back, Aimee, he loves you too much to stay away.'

To this Aimee smiled, so Darren smiled back.

Sad and troubled though they were, Aimee and Darren managed to carry on with life as normally as possible. It wasn't until four days later that they were reminded of the incident. They were strolling down Turner Avenue on the way back home from another boring day at school when they heard a terrible uproar from down a side street. Cautiously they followed the sound towards the commotion.

'Rover!' cried Aimee. 'Here boy!'

See,' exclaimed Darren, 'I told you he'd come back.'

Aimee wrapped her arms round the big brown Labrador.

Shelley Doyle (13)
The Garendon High School, Loughborough

A Day In The Life Of A Tree

I saw the sun rise this morning. On the horizon, just above the city. A vivid orange globe ascending into the morning sky like a porpoise surfacing to breathe.

Gradually I stretched my branches, soaking up the melting rays that beamed down on the sleepy village of Thistleberry.

It's not often that exciting events occur in a place like this, not for me anyway. The primary school had its annual sports day yesterday and the vicar's wife bore a beautiful little girl on Saturday, but my life is tedious and my days lengthy and uneventful.

It's spring again. My little buds are blossoming into vibrantly-coloured flowers and the bees have spent many a day hovering purposefully around them. Blackbirds and robins, sparrows and thrushes, they're all dancing gleefully on the green, expecting their breakfast to emerge from the dewy, jade lawn.

There go the children, skipping merrily off to school. Many of them stop and play about me, mums hurrying their little ones up the road.

Ah, peace and quiet again, just the distant humming of a tractor on the fields. Is that a spot of rain I felt? Oh yes, it's very refreshing. I could do with some water for my roots, I'm parched. It's getting heavier, my leaves are sodden. Was that thunder I heard? A flash flickered before me, lighting up the sky. Close. Closer. I'm hit, ablaze, burnt to the core. I will always be the tree where the lightning struck. Charred, forever silhouetted against the sky ...

Sophie Easton (13)
The Garendon High School, Loughborough

Kathy's Nightmare

Kathy took two brave steps forward and cautiously peered around the corner of the dark, dirty house. Carefully she crept to the bottom of the long, winding stairs. In front of her was a full length dusty mirror. Written in the dust: 'Look behind you'. She wiped the dust quickly and anxiously off the mirror. Frightened, she stood face to face with the reflection of her worst nightmare. Her head rotated automatically. Her eyes widened, as she glared at this mysterious figure through her soft, blonde hair.

Shivers sprinted up her spine, the hairs on her back stood up like an army standing to attention. She was like an ice cube, cold, frozen. The monstrous figure leapt out of the shadows and attempted to pounce on its prey. Kathy, breathing heavily, rolled across the floor and headed towards the door. In a matter of seconds she got to the brown painted door. She noticed it had a plank of large, new wood nailed into it. Swiftly she turned around, she saw a scaly, red face bound towards her. His eyes were daring, mischievous, glowing and harmful. She stood motionless and saw it emerge from the darkness and sneakily approach her. She snatched the chair beside her and threw it at the mystifying creature. The chair, with now only three dented legs, was flung through the window giving Kathy the chance of making an escape. Hopeful, she rushed to the smashed window and glanced behind her. Was her nightmare finally over?

Kelly Bruce (13)
The Garendon High School, Loughborough

Twenty-Seven Years Of Solitude - One Day In The Life Of Nelson Mandela

The dawn breaks. I wake and labour in the quarries, endure torrents of abuse against my race and people, day after day. An existence of torpor, toil and excruciating pain. Our backs run with irrepressible rivulets of perspiration. Suffering stoically, we shed sweat and tears for a nation. We labour for the rich soils, the lush grass, the mountains' crooked crags, the rolling hills nestled in valleys, the bold sunset which transforms its surroundings into a palette of vivid crimson and vermilion hues. I labour for my beloved country, whose beauty is suffocated by evil. Her people suffer under the oppression of discrimination. Her rivers run red with blood shed by those courageous enough to protest systematic persecution. Yet, beyond the walls of my prison, I sense the intensity of flames burning white-hot in the hearts of my people, a passion to break free from the shackles of corruption.

After a gruelling day's work I lie in my cell, hearing the scuffling of rats amongst the straw, and dream of a country whose cavernous rift between black and white races is closed. I dream of people of all ethnic origins working together, children playing together, the elderly talking together - a rainbow nation. A coalition and collaboration of all races, to form an invincible, united structure on which to build and improve the country, my country. I sleep, knowing that as I suffer, I stoke the fire in my people's hearts and lead them in the arduous struggle for freedom.

Leonie Amarasekara (12)
The Garendon High School, Loughborough

The Red-Eyed Mystery

There is an unexplained mystery, the mystery of a tall, dark figure with reflective red eyes on his shoulders, with black wings on his back, who can predict the future and tell you what you are doing when you are not even close.

This all started in the year of 1966 in Point Pleasant, West Virginia. Sightings were reported, the most well-known one and the alleged first sighting on November 15th when two couples were driving along in their cars when they spotted two red lights (or eyes) at a World War II TNT factory site. They stopped the car and noticed that there was a silhouette of a tall, dark figure with wings attached to his back. Terrified, the couples started their cars again and carried on driving, but further on, going down a road, they saw it again, standing there, looking at them. It took off and followed them to the city. They reported the sighting but that wasn't the only one that there was.

There were many more sightings to come, the next few were spotted by the TNT site again, or even flying above it. But they weren't all there, it had been noticed all over the world, even in England, and worst of all, in recent years.

Not everybody believes in the creature, some people think that it is just a myth, a figure of the imagination, a made-up story. This creature which has an eerie presence around it is called the Mothman.

Beth Garton (13)
The Garendon High School, Loughborough

My Short Story
(Inspired by ideas from the book 'Stone Cold' by Robert Swindells)

I spent as long as I possibly could in the café. I'd been sitting in the warmth, sipping the same cup of coffee for an hour and a half and no one had realised. In the end, after another thirty minutes, a polite waitress asked me to leave.

For the rest of the day I wandered around the busy streets of London and at six o'clock I began my nightly search for a doorway to doss down in for the night. About ten minutes into my search an empty doorway came into view. It was an old entrance to a derelict building and it was clean and wide enough to lay down my sleeping bag. I set down my stuff and lay down in the doorway.

That night was my second night sleeping on the streets of London. I couldn't stand living at home. My mum and stepdad were always arguing and him and I didn't get on. What made it worse was his drinking problem. When he had been drinking he had a very bad temper, so that's why I left.

As I was just about to go to sleep someone suddenly shouted my name. My mum was standing at the other end of the street with a smile spreading across her face. I froze, I didn't know what to do. I felt happy seeing my mum again but I did not want to go back and live a life of hell.

Naomi Warrington (13)
The Garendon High School, Loughborough

The Legend Of Sawney Bean!

Hundreds of years ago lived a man named Sawney Bean. He lived with his wife and many children in a sea cave on the Ayrshire coast. Sawney was the head of a strange family. They were very poor and to survive they did the most unspeakable things.

Sawney was born in the late 14th century in a small town near Edinburgh. He was idle and dishonest. He ran away with a woman as nasty as he was. As they had no money they lived in a cave on the Ayrshire coast. To support themselves they robbed and murdered travellers and locals. After killing them they ate their flesh.

As time passed, Sawney's family got larger ever year. As hundreds of people continued to go missing every year, the finger began to point towards the Beans. Unwanted bodies were usually tossed into the sea and floated ashore further down the coast.

As Sawney's family grew, they began to attack larger groups. Within their twenty-five year reign they killed about 1,000 women, men and children. They were finally discovered when a couple returning home from a trip fell right into the Beans' trap. Fortunately the man escaped but his wife died as she fell off her horse and was ripped to shreds. The man told King James I who sent 400 bloodhounds to find the Beans.

Sawney Bean's cave is thought to be at Bennane on the South Ayrshire coast.

Annie Kirk (13)
The Garendon High School, Loughborough

A Day In The Life Of Harry The Hippo

Harry Gets Lost

'Wake up, Harry,' said a faraway voice.

Harry, the young hippo, opened his eyes to find his mother, Bertha, staring at him.

'Come on, Harry, we're moving today,' Bertha nudged him and moved away.

We are? thought Harry as he got up. 'I'm thirsty,' he said and wandered over to the river for a drink.

'Come on, let's go,' called Bertha.

Harry joined his mother and they began to walk. They came to the edge of the forest.

'Stay close, Harry,' warned Bertha, heading into the trees, Harry a little behind her.

They had been walking for a while when Bertha pointed out a magpie's nest.

'Look Harry, a magpie's nest. I'll bet it's full of jewels,' Bertha looked up at it.

There was a sudden squawk and a large white and blue bird was sitting on top of the nest. It cocked its head to one side and stared at Harry. Harry turned around to find Bertha gone! Panicking, he rushed around. Where was she? It was already getting dark. The trees loomed above him, their eerie branches stretching towards him.

'Mummy! Mummy, where are you?' he shouted desperately. He came to a clearing and lay down. Harry sighed. 'I'm lost,' he mumbled.

'Yes you are,' said a familiar voice.

Harry turned around. 'Mummy!' he cried.

'I told you to stay close, didn't I?' smiled Bertha.

Then they set off together, Harry riding on his mother's back, to their new home.

Nikki Hoyle (12)
The Garendon High School, Loughborough

A Day In The Life Of A Cat

My day begins when I wake up early - about two o'clock in the morning, when all my humans are in bed. I then stroll outside to the loo. Once I'm done, I have a friendly chat with the family of blackbirds who live behind my backyard. Sometimes an old member of their family asks me if I can end his/her woe by ... well, you know! But then the human shouts at me as if I've done something wrong and they lock me out of my house - yes, my own house!

Later in the day one of the humans does an odd ritual - in fact, three times a day. Something gets pulled out of the cupboard and emptied into a small, silver dish. Then the human starts to sing.

'Tigger! Tigger!'

I'd really like to know who this 'Tigger' is. It can't be me. My name is Prince Charles Edward of Fish and Chips, so it must be one of the humans. Eventually the human stops and sulks away. Then, standing in the place of where my human was dancing is a bowl of flavoured food!

Afterwards I snoop around my territory (everywhere I dare to go) fighting off intruders. My humans would be overrun with animals if it wasn't for me, but they never thank me! I would kick them out of my house if they didn't create food and provide a great place to sit. Now it's time for a nap. Mmmmm ... that's comfy ... it's a 'purrrrfect' life!

Mark Boyde-Shaw (13)
The Garendon High School, Loughborough

A Day In The Life Of ...

Every morning I am awoken by the sun's gleaming rays sneaking themselves into my tiny, compact room.

My name is Hope and I am a 3-year-old unicorn. I live under the rainbow far above the clouds in my master's grand castle.

Every day my master sends me out to do chores. He doesn't care about me or my 2 friends, Love and Trust, for he only cares about his precious gold. He never rewards us for carrying out his requests, he just punishes us for not getting the amount of gold he is expecting, which is usually carried out by a whip or a knife. But still we proceed to obey his every command, as we are in fear of being tortured or even killed.

My master is a giant. He has a gruesome-looking face, evil, slanting, red eyes which we are terrified to look at directly. He also has a scruffy beard and long black hair. He is a terrible man, very greedy, and he doesn't love anybody except himself.

On an average day after we have woken up, we begin our chores. We fly several miles to get to the gold mines. We then start digging and we take back as much as our weak bodies can hold at a time. When we get home we are greeted by a bellowing rage as we probably haven't brought back enough.

One day we will have had enough and we will stand up to him. Yes, one day ...

Sofie Bunce (13)
The Garendon High School, Loughborough

Sergeant Roberts' Last Stand

Shambling towards Sergeant Roberts and his men, the aliens were just a giant mass of tentacles and mutated flesh. Their slimy, colourless and grotesque bodies seemed to slide along the ground. The disciplined volleys of lasers from Roberts' men cut down many, but there were many more.

'Remember men, we can't let them take this power plant or we're done for,' said Roberts.

This was true, if the plant fell then the power to the city would be out and the turrets would go offline. At the moment the sergeant and his men were sheltering behind an office block. The aliens didn't usually have weapons but lately they'd got smarter.

The two FAM's laser cannons were blowing chunks out of the mutant crowd. Originally there had been three of the armoured behemoths but one had been taken out by a lucky shot to its power core. The pilot had skilfully driven it into the mass of aliens where its power cell exploded with explosive results.

'We need to retreat,' said Roberts.

'Retreat!' yelled Corporal Stone.

'Goodbye Stone,' said Robert, a plasma grenade in each hand.

'What are you doing?'

'Don't ask, just get out,' Roberts ordered.

The aliens had reached a highly flammable secondary power tube. Roberts ran right into the mass of aliens. One hit him, sending him flying into the tube, his vision darkened. The aliens closed in for the kill.

'See you in Hell,' he shouted as he pressed the detonators.

Alex Shephard (13)
The Garendon High School, Loughborough

A Day In The Life Of My Dog

8.15pm   Actually got fed. (First time in 23 hours, not that I'm complaining - wouldn't dare!)

8.30pm   Lovely dinner/tea, had beef covered in gravy. (Well, how was I supposed to know it was his lunch?)

9pm   Hear a funny noise at the gate. I'll go investigate.

9.01pm   Nothing there, must have been that dim rat scavenging about for any guinea pig food that's been dropped. Doesn't he know that there's a rat trap?

10pm   So sleepy, must sleep ... *yawn!*

1am   Wake up to a squirrel throwing acorns at me. *Bark! Bark!* Ha, the beggar's gone now!

7.15am   Long, tall thing standing above me. Looks like ... oh, it's just the master wanting to take me for a walk. Yippee!

7.45am   Walk was great, even killed a pheasant. Master wasn't pleased but what does he know? I mean, they wear fluffy cotton things, why don't they be like us dogs - bare!

10am   Walk around kennel for a bit.

10.01am   Still walking around kennel (bored)!

Midday   Car pulls up and a dog jumps out. Well, I thought it was but it was the next-door neighbour. Oops ... they shouldn't wear fur coats. (I'll let her have that sleeve when I've dug it up!)

8pm   Lovely tea, chicken, gravy and half a Yorkshire pudding (must be on a diet).

9pm   Sleeping, I think. Night. *Zzz.* (Am I asleep yet?)

Becki Mottershaw (12)
The Phoenix School, Telford

The Terrifying Ghost Story

Lucy tripped over a twig. She was in the middle of the woods. She was alone. Her brother had walked off that day because she'd made him cry. *Oh well,* she thought, *he will live.* Because of what Lucy had done, she was the one who was made to go and find him. She told her mum that she was scared, but she made him cry so she would go by herself. In the woods Lucy saw an old cottage, it was wet and cold. It freaked her out but she had to find her brother so she thought hard. *Would he have gone in there?* He'd said he loved old cottages. She slowly opened the door. There was a pale girl in there. *Could it be his girlfriend? No, he had left her.*

Lucy screamed. It was a ghost, but there was a boy, it looked like her brother. It was him! He was hiding in the corner. He was dead. He was going to kill her. She ran but she kept tripping over her laces. The howling noise that she'd heard before kept going on. It was a wolf. Her brother was still chasing her. He got her and tied her up on a tree. All the family are dead now. They are all alone!

Sharese Pritchard (12)
The Phoenix School, Telford

War! Ants Vs Termites

'Sgt Tiny, get that cake!' It was a fridge raid. The commanding ant was General Titch. 'Tiny, get your men to that cake. LT Small, 5 men to each sausage, men, move it out!'

The Queen Ants Royal Army was marching on the kitchen floor towards the ant colony. The army was almost at the ant hill entry when … the neighbour's house cat, Mr Whiskers, had seen the ants. They ran to the hole but Private Mini had dropped his strawberry.

'Run, Mini!' cried his friend, Private Inch.

Mini picked up the strawberry and began to run towards Inch as Mr Whiskers closed in.

'Jump, Mini!' Inch screamed from the entrance.

Mini jumped at the ant hill, just avoiding Mr Whiskers and bumping into Inch. They both slid down the ant hill and thudded at the bottom.

'Thanks Inch!' thanked Mini.

'No problem,' Inch murmured.

Mini looked around at the ant colony. It had hundreds of mud skyscrapers, small shops, bars, all in an underground cavern. Inch and Mini went to the bar.

'Hey Inch, do you think we'll have to fight in the war between ants and termites?' asked Mini.

'Nah, they want experienced soldiers,' answered Inch.

'Yeah.' It was Rocket and his cronies, Dumb and Dumber. 'The army doesn't want privates in a war.'

Suddenly the three fainted.

'Whoa!' shouted Kunchi, the kung fu grasshopper.

'Hi Kunchi,' greeted Mini.

The next day the three ants were put in the war. Who won? Well, who had the bug spray?

Liam Clyne (11)
The Phoenix School, Telford

Paris' Star
(An extract)

Once, when in the world all love was shot through arrows and everyone loved each other, Venus, goddess of love, thought as long as she lived she would never be alone without her beloved husband, Paris, prince of Troy. Until one day when jealous Aëëtes returned from a far-off place that was never spoken of. The man with no heart was envious of Paris.

Venus was the most beautiful woman on Mount Olympus - her hair was like pure silk woven by the most skilful gods of all time and her lips had been kissed by the deep red rose shining in the sunlight. Her eyes glistened like gleaming blue sapphires; but Aëëtes was the opposite to the beautiful Venus. He was the most ungrateful man and did not care about anyone else but himself. Whatever he wanted, somehow he got it, even if it meant breaking someone's heart. He lived at the deepest, darkest corner of the world. Here no one ever dared to step one foot onto the ground. No creatures of any kind lived there except the slaves that worked for Aëëtes. All the trees had died and stood there in the forest. The grass was blades of the sharpest knives, each one sharp enough to slice through a bone and destroy it.

Aëëtes never truly loved anyone. His heart was as bitter as ice and all he gained was to fall in love. But anger overgrew him and evil overtook his life. When he touched anything with warmth and love it turned to dust in his fingers. Aëëtes was jealous of Paris and wanted Venus for his own.

Paris was the most handsome man on Mount Olympus. His hair was long, thick and wavy locks and was the colour of the brightest ray of sun. His face looked like it had been created by angels. His tall, thin body was what any woman would die for.

Paris and Venus were walking along the beautiful enchanted gardens, gazing at the marvellous flowers and the exotic plants that grew high above the clouds, while in a segmented bush stood Aëëtes, full of jealousy. It was as if he were a tiger ready to pounce on his prey, but the thing that made him nearly burst was when Venus and Paris kissed.

Clearly he was concocting a plan to trick Venus into coming with him. He thought if he could disguise himself as Paris, maybe, just maybe, he might be able to have Venus at last to belong to him. He knew it would work ...

Melissa Hollies (12)
Woodhouse Middle School, Stoke-on-Trent

How The Kangaroo Got Its Spring
(An extract)

In the loneliness of Australia, there was a kangaroo called Joseph but everyone called him Joey, except his parents who were a little old-fashioned!

It was the warmest day of the year so far, so Joey went to the waterhole to collect water for his family. While walking along, it was then he first saw a group of wild rabbits hopping away into the bushes. He thought he would ask Mother Nature if he could have a spring in his step, feeling that he would love to be as good as they were and excited at the prospect of bouncing from place to place.

As he collected water, a robust-looking rabbit hopped towards the waterhole for a drink. Joey began to question the rabbit.

'Do you like being able to jump every minute, every day?'

The rabbit answered, 'Yes, it's fabulous. You can reach and see things which are higher. It's a great advantage!'

Joey thought that the rabbit was beginning to boast.

'I really don't know what I'd do without a spring in my step, in my step,' the rabbit continued.

'Well, I really don't care, I mean, why would I want to have a spring in my step?' Joey lied, but he knew deep inside he wanted it. 'Just by any chance, do you know where to find Mother Nature?' Joey asked (completely changing the subject).

The rabbit's jaw nearly dropped to the ground in shock. 'Of course I know!' the rabbit carried on boasting. 'Everyone does. It's by the lake that glistens by day and night outside the town. You know where I mean, by the dark cave?'

'Ah, I understand now, thank you so much,' Joey replied. *I must go and see Mother Nature first thing tomorrow,* he thought.

Sally Brown (11)
Woodhouse Middle School, Stoke-on-Trent

How The Rain Became
(An extract)

Apollo was sitting on the sun reciting his new poem. He lived in the most unusual place; somewhere where no other god or goddess lived. He enjoyed his home on the sun and loved the peace and quiet, the beauty and loveliness of the sun and its flowers, birds and trees which shared his home with him. It was the happiest place. Everywhere it was seen, people were glad, it even made the planets happy when the glorious rays shone down on the surface of it. Rough or smooth, upset or angry, the sun brightened everything and everyone. Animals gathered round from all over the Earth to witness the spectacular rays the sun displayed. Everything on the planet Earth was peaceful, the clouds stopped like statues not to block the sun in full glory, the living creatures were in a period of harmony, wars stopped, hunting stopped and everything was still.

Pluto, the god of the Underworld, hated this happiness and for several days he set out to destroy the sun and Apollo with it. He considered many cunning plots and finally he thought of the best idea he had ever come across. He was going to destroy the sun and make it rain forever. Pluto thought that if he killed Apollo, the sun would disappear because the sun was in his soul! For a long while, he carefully corrected his plans, going over and over them. Nothing could possibly go wrong ...

One afternoon, when Apollo was resting in a fine field of royal red poppies, Hermes, the messenger of the gods, came from Mount Olympus with news from the Underworld. Hermes took a while to say this because it was not good news.

Apollo had a short temper and hated gods for some things they said, even though it wasn't their fault. Apollo especially didn't like Hermes; whenever Apollo's day was going brilliantly, Hermes was always there to spoil it with *bad* news. Hermes did not like being so hated and so only came to the sun when the news was good or really bad. This time the news was really awful, more terrifying than any other news Apollo had heard.

'Apollo, I am afraid I have some rather bad news for you; I'm extremely sorry but Pluto has a plot to destroy you and the sun. The message came in this morning from Persephone, she said she found the papers with the plan on hidden by the slave quarters!'

'I see,' exclaimed Apollo, getting more angry by every word he said. 'I'll sort this out!'

Apollo was trying to stay calm, but Hermes could see this calmness wouldn't last. He was right. Apollo was so angry he even threatened to kill Pluto and he was serious. Hermes decided to leave and tell Zeus, the head of all the gods and goddesses!

Meanwhile, on the planet Earth, it was intensely hot, people were getting angry with the sun's heat. The heat was the anger of Apollo.

Apollo ordered his faithful flying horse to take him to the home of Pluto, the Underworld. When his horse was there, Apollo found Pluto and a fight broke out!

After a long while, Apollo had won the battle - Pluto was killed.

Natalie Yates (12)
Woodhouse Middle School, Stoke-on-Trent

How The Lily Became

Many moons ago, there lived a young nymph called Lily. This certain young nymph had a favourite flower which grew down by the riverbank. Nobody knew the name of this flower for the goddess of flowers, Flora, had passed away.

Lily had a best friend called Violet. She was a pretty young nymph who lived next door. One day, Violet was cleaning Lily's house as she did every day (because Lily made her) as Lily sunbathed in the sweltering midday sun.

Violet suddenly came rushing out. 'That's it, I can't take it anymore. I clean and polish your house while you lie out here like a lizard. I'm leaving the village.'

'What do you mean?' Lily asked.

'What do I mean? I mean you're treating me like your slave. You make me do your housework every day and in summer you make me do your gardening.'

'What do you mean? This is what friends are supposed to do for each other!' Lily replied.

'No they're not, Lily. Friends are supposed to be nice to each other. I'm leaving the kingdom!'

'Fine then, be like that, but don't come running to me when all those wild animals out there get you.'

Just as Violet was walking away into the distance a loud voice bellowed from the sky, one that only Lily could hear.

'Lily, you have betrayed yours and Violet's friendship. I can't believe you would be that mean, especially to your best friend.'

'Please forgive me, Sir, I didn't mean to upset her,' she pleaded.

'No, Lily, you have an hour to find her and make friends again or I will turn you into a flower. Now go and find her!'

Lily set off to find her. Eventually, with five minutes to spare, she found Violet sitting on a rock talking to Pan.

'Could you give us a minute, Pan? We need to talk, urgently.'

'Yes, of course, Lily,' replied Pan.

'Can I sit down, Violet?' Lily asked sympathetically.

'Yeah, sure, take a seat,' said Violet. 'There is something I have been wanting to tell you.'

'Yes, me too,' said Lily. 'I've come to say …'

Just as those words were spoken, history was made. Lily became a flower growing next to the rock where Lily and Violet once sat. Now people call that very flower a lily.

And that's how the lily became.

Georgina Hollinshead (11)
Woodhouse Middle School, Stoke-on-Trent